HEAVEN TOUCHING EARTH

Heaven Touching Earth

DAILY SCRIPTURE VERSES AND REFLECTIONS

Michele Mason

Heaven Touching Earth Books

Contents

Copyright

Other books by Michele Mason:

Fun with Felt: How to make Advent and Lenten calendars

More Fun with Felt: How to make a liturgical year calendar

Fun with Bible Stories: A"Hands-on" book designed to teach young children the alphabet through Bible stories

The previous books were self-published and printed. Contact heaventouchingearthbooks@gmail.com to find out more.

Scripture verses are quoted from:
The Catholic Edition of the Revised Standard Version of the Bible, copyright 1965,
1966 by the Division of Christian Education of the National Council of the Churches of Christ in the United States of America

Heaven Touching Earth: Daily Scripture Verses and Reflections and its related characters logos are trademark and copyright
2019-2020 of Michele Mason

heaventouchingearthbooks@gmail.com
This book was begun in 2005, "The Year of the Eucharist"

Printed in the United States of America

Dedication

For Mom and Dad. Thank you for raising me in the faith and for the constant love you've given me.

For Grandpa and Grandma Bieker. Thank you for the inspiration of your quiet, prayerful lives. You showed me that a person can live a quiet life and still make a big difference in the world.

For my husband, Mike, and all our precious kiddos: Amber Lyn, Emmalee Marie, Erik James, Kimberly Anne, Nicole Michele, Alison Elizabeth, Maria Clare, Luke Michael, Eva Rose, and our babies in heaven, Amy Agnes, Abby Esther, John Michael, and Anthony John Paul. You have taught me how to love and have blessed me with so much love.

Introduction

I invite you into my life. Journey with me and recognize the presence of God in the good times and bad. Recall the joys and sufferings in your own life and discover how God is with us as Heaven Touches Earth every day.

In our lives, we all receive gifts from God each day. These gifts are sometimes very subtle, and they often go unnoticed as we go about our busy lives. Sometimes the gifts are ignored. Sometimes it is hard to see the gift in the midst of a struggle we may be having, but we will eventually see it if we keep ourselves open to God's grace and spend time in silence. It is in these quiet moments that we can recognize the graces and gifts given to us by God and can grow closer to Him every day.

In some of these stories, I have opened my heart and shared things I really would rather hide away. However, I have shared some very private things in hopes that they will help someone in a struggle they may be having so they will remember that God is with them and that there is always hope. I have also shared joys that I hope others will see mirrored in their lives.

Dear Reader, you can read this book as simply that, a book,

or you can meditate on the Bible verses and reflections, one each day for 40 days, thinking of how God has touched your own life. Seek out other Bible verses that you can identify with and take comfort in. Think of the times you have seen God's grace and love in your life and thank Him. When we are full of thankfulness for God's gifts, our focus is on the good in the world and not the bad. If we stay in this thankful spirit, then we can move forward, love God with all our hearts, and do what He is calling us to do.

- In the reflection sections in this book, you will sometimes find action items. These are faith steps, things you can do that will help you grow in faith. Of course, there are many things you can do to grow closer to the Lord, these are just a few suggestions of things I have done in my own life over the years that have brought me closer to God.

It is my hope that you use this book to reflect on your own experiences in life, perhaps writing them down, and meditating on how God has brought heaven to earth in your own life.

Like Mary, the Mother of Jesus, took everything to heart, let us do the same.

"But Mary kept all these things, pondering them in her heart."
Luke 2:19

Day 1

Grandma's Goodbye

"For since we believe that Jesus died and rose again, even so, through Jesus, God will bring with Him those who have fallen asleep; For this we declare to you by the Word of the Lord, that we who are alive, who are left until the coming of the Lord, shall not precede those who have fallen asleep."
1 Thess. 4:14-15

"Grandma died?" I asked, stunned.

"Yes," my mom replied. *"She just passed away a few hours ago."*

My mind drifted back to earlier that evening when I was sitting with my husband and children in the living room watching a television program. In the middle of the show, I had a sudden feeling that my grandma needed my prayers. I stopped and said a couple of prayers for her. I went about the rest of the evening not thinking much about it. When I received that phone call from my mom, I asked her what time Grandma had passed away. Mom told me and I was shocked!

It was the exact same time I'd had the feeling earlier.

While I don't know if Grandma was saying goodbye to me, or if perhaps she needed some extra prayers, I do know something very amazing and wonderful had happened. God had given me a glimpse of the eternal. No, I didn't see any great visions or signs, there was just a feeling in my soul, a connection between this life and the next. How easily I could have ignored the feeling to pray for her. I was tempted to do so at the time and say a prayer later. How glad I am that I didn't ignore the feeling to pray.

I don't know why I was the one to receive this wonderful goodbye present. Perhaps the answer is the inspiration for this book, then again maybe not. Perhaps the answer will be revealed to me in the future, but then again maybe not. It may just be one of the heavenly "kisses" we all receive throughout our lives when heaven touches earth.

This encounter with God, my grandma, and heaven so many years ago made me more aware that there is a profound connection between us and the spiritual world. We are surrounded by the spiritual world, encompassed in it. We cannot see it, but we get little glimpses of it in our daily lives.

We can experience God with us and heaven on earth every day if we just open our hearts, search for our Lord, and ask Him for the graces and gifts He wishes to send us. His heart is open, waiting for us to call on Him.

Reflection

Have you ever felt or experienced something spiritual that seemed like coincidence that you couldn't explain? How did it affect you? What "heavenly kiss" have you received from God lately?

Day 2

A Pack of Doublemint Gum

"With all your heart honor your father; and do not forget the birth pangs of your mother. Remember that through your parents you were born; and what can you give back to them that equals their gift to you?" Sirach 7:27-28

Daddy hugs are the best. When my dad enfolded me in his arms, as a child or as an adult, I felt all the worries of the world fade away. I felt safe and protected. I felt loved.

My dad was an amazing man. He was a loving dad. He was always kind and fair to others, and he was a great example of how to live with faith.

When I was little, I had this special tradition with my dad on Father's Day. I would give him a pack of Doublemint gum as a gift. This tradition continued until he died in 2018. It all started when I was a child and I wanted to get him something special for Father's Day. I had noticed that whenever he came home from work each day and emptied his pockets, he always had a pack of gum in the pile. For Father's Day that year, I bought him a pack of his favorite kind. Dad took his pack of Father's Day gum and he shared it with all of us kids. To me, that is the epitome of fatherhood. My dad gave his all. He gave us the sacrifice of working 12 hours a day, Monday through Saturday, over 70 hours a week, so we could be provided for. He gave us his faith by taking us to Mass each week and praying the rosary with us. He gave us his all, down to his last pack of Doublemint gum. That is fatherhood! That is a gift from God.

My mom was (and is) a loving mom. She gave totally of herself to her family. Over the years, my mom made sacrifice after sacrifice for us kids. She would buy us clothes and the things we needed while she wore the same dresses for 20 years. She took care of us when we were sick, read to us, fixed us amazing meals, comforted us when we were feeling down, and so much more. Even though we are all adults now, we still know she is there for us. That is a gift from God. That is God's unselfish presence.

I remember some fun times with my mom, like having water fights with her when doing the dishes together. There were always baby bottle nipples to wash from my little sister's bottles, and we would fill the nipples with water and spray each other and laugh and laugh.

Heaven touches earth when God gives us the gift of our parents. As adults, we can choose to focus on what our parents did wrong in raising us or we can thank God for the gift of our parents and remember the things they did that were loving and giving.

"Hear, my son, your father's instruction, and reject not your mother's teaching; for they are a fair garland for your head, and pendants for your neck." Proverbs 1:8-9

Reflection

What was (is) your earthly father like? Did he make many sacrifices for you? Even if your earthly father didn't live up to your expectations or if you didn't experience a father's love like you should have, God is waiting to be that perfect Father. He IS that perfect Father. Go to Him. Spiritually feel yourself enfolded in His embrace and experience a father's love.

Day 3

Everyday Encounters Through Nature

"Therefore I tell you, do not be anxious about your life, what you shall eat or what you shall drink, nor about your body, what you shall put on. Is not life more than food, and the body more than clothing? Look at the birds of the air; they neither sow nor reap nor gather into barns, and yet your heavenly Father feeds them. Are you not of more value than they?" Matthew 6:25

Encountering God in nature is one of my favorite ways to learn more about God and experience His love and care. Breathing in the crisp mountain air, feeling the warm sun on my face and the gentle breeze on my skin, and being in the quiet of nature just brings peace to my heart and joy to my soul. Hiking through the mountains is the best!

"Every day that passes, I fall more desperately in love with the mountains....I am ever more determined to climb the mountains, to

scale the mighty peaks, to feel that pure joy which can only be felt in the mountains." Blessed Pier Giorgio Frassati

In my younger years, I used to go fishing with my dad. These times I hold dear in my heart. They are memories of peace and solitude. Dad and I didn't have to talk. We were quiet most of the time, enjoying each other's company, enjoying nature, and silently talking to God.

When I was a college student, I enjoyed going to early morning classes. Was I crazy? Maybe. The walk to class was so peaceful with very few students up that early in the morning. It was then I discovered that the simple sparrow is my absolute favorite bird. It's not the prettiest bird, and there is nothing about it that makes it stand out from the others, but as I walked to class in the morning, these simple little birds kept me company. As I walked to class, they would greet me with their happy little chirps. They would hop, hop, hop around and I would watch them with great joy. Some days I wished I could become a sparrow for a while and fly away with them and forget about the worries of life.

When I moved to California and eventually got married and had a family of my own, I was so busy taking care of my family, I didn't realize how much I had missed being out in nature until I was in my 40's. I missed the beauty. I missed the peace. I missed the closeness I felt with God.

My first hint that I needed outdoor time in my life was when Fr. Timothy, my spiritual director, told me I needed to do something fun. I tried different things, but it wasn't until I went back into nature that I rediscovered this wonderful gift of God's creation that I had forgotten.

"Let the heavens be glad, and let the earth rejoice; let the sea roar, and all that fills it; let the field exult, and everything in it! Then shall all the trees of the wood sing for joy." Psalm 96:11-12

Reflection

What is a gift in nature that brings joy to your soul? Where do you best love being in nature? The forest? The mountains? The beach? How does being in nature bring you closer to God?

- Faith step: Plan a time to encounter God in nature.

Day 4

I'm Going on an Adventure!

"For God did not give us a spirit of timidity but a spirit of power and love and self-control." 2 Timothy 1:7

Like Bilbo Baggins, my brother Mike unknowingly taught me that life is an adventure. When he went to have his tonsils out, Mike told Mom that it was going to be an adventure. I decided at that point in my life to take on that attitude, always. The good things that happen in life, the bad things that happen, I would look at them all as an adventure.

Looking back, my life has been an amazing journey, showered with good times and bad, a grand adventure. I didn't realize it in my younger years, but God's hand was guiding me all the way, in all the decisions I made, in the places I went. Did I always make the right decisions? Definitely not, but God was with me to lead me back along the path when I strayed.

When I was 5 years old, my adventurous spirit reared its

head. I decided I was a big girl and I was going to take my sister and go visit our neighbor across the street (whom I didn't know). I only remember bits and pieces of what happened. I recall knocking on the neighbor's door and a nice, middle-aged lady answered. I told her that we came over to visit. She asked me if my mom knew we were there. *"Yes,"* I lied. She invited us in, and they gave us a tour of their house. I don't recall anything about the tour, but I do remember when we came up from downstairs, she gave us cookies. After we ate the cookies, I told her we'd better be getting home and we all said, *"Goodbye."* The next memory I had was crying on my bunk bed, not knowing why I got a spanking. I didn't know it, but my mom and sister were frantically searching for us because they didn't know where we were. They looked everywhere, including the nearby river. I didn't understand what I did wrong until I was older.

"I think I'm quite ready for another adventure!"
Bilbo Baggins in *Lord of the Rings,* J.R.R. Tolkien

I had many other adventures throughout my childhood, but my next grand adventure would happen during my college years when I was an Art major at Fort Hays State University in Hays, Kansas. One summer day, my friend Mary Alice and I headed to the state fair to see the Beach Boys. My thoughts at that concert were of a warm sunny beach, no more winter, and Disneyland. (Brian Wilson of the Beach Boys waved to me, by the way.) Three years into college, I was ready for a change. After that concert, I was California

Dreamin'. This small-town girl was ready to get away from rural towns and head for the city, action, and fun! I was ready for a grand adventure!

I applied for the National Student Exchange Program and got accepted at California State University, San Bernardino. I was both excited and scared to leave Kansas. I said goodbye to my friends and my boyfriend and headed to California in my little stick shift Mazda. My parents didn't want me to go alone, so they drove their van and I took my little car.

While in college, I started working at The Early Learning Tree Day Care Center. I absolutely loved teaching the little 3- and 4-year-old children. They were so full of life, so fun, and so very entertaining! I felt called to be a teacher.

Two years later, I graduated with a B.A. in Art from CSUSB. I wondered what I would do with an art degree. (It seems like I should have been thinking of that all along...) Thankfully, I got accepted into a teaching internship program at CSUSB and passed the National Teacher's Exam. I earned the extra credits I needed to be a teacher and I was hired on at Fontana Unified School District as a 2nd-grade teacher, another great adventure! I absolutely loved teaching. The staff was amazing, and the kids were great.

I'm getting a bit ahead of myself in this story since I haven't introduced my husband yet, but you'll hear about him soon. One of the greatest adventures I have been on is that of motherhood. The reality of giving birth to my first child, this innocent baby dependent totally on me, woke me out of my selfish reality of me, myself, and I. The recovery from birth, the sleepless nights, everything I was going through was exhausting, new, and scary. And yet it was amazing and beautiful. My baby girl was amazing and beautiful.

Developing my relationship with God is the grandest adventure I've been on. As I draw closer to Him through prayer, through suffering, through discovering and following His will, He opens my heart to know Him and to love Him a tiny bit better each day. Each encounter, each gift of love He gives to me, opens my heart to a taste of the ultimate joy and wonder I will experience in heaven. He gives me a burning desire to love Him and to be with Him forever.

"To fall in love with God is the greatest romance;
To seek Him, the greatest adventure;
To find Him, the greatest human achievement."
St. Augustine of Hippo

Reflection

Heaven touches earth in the adventures in our lives.

What amazing adventures have you been on in your lifetime? Did these adventures bring you closer to God? What adventures would you like to still go on?

Day 5

A Broken Heart

"The Lord is near to the broken-hearted, and saves the crushed in spirit." Psalm 34:18

When I was accepted into the National Student Exchange Program and moved to California at age 21, I had my first real taste of suffering. My family drove out with me to help me move but when it was time for them to leave, reality set in and I knew I would be alone. After 21 years of being surrounded by love—a mother and father who loved me, six amazing siblings who did as well, and many great friends—I would be totally alone. I was devastated.

As my family got settled in their van and got ready to leave, my 5-year-old sister, Chrissy, started crying and said she wanted to stay with me. I cried. After they left, sadness overtook me like a black cloud in my soul. I sat in my dorm room, crying, with a heart that truly felt broken. (I discovered then what the words "broken heart" really meant.)

Moving to California had been my own decision, but since I tend to be rather impulsive at times and don't always think before acting, I didn't realize how much I would miss my family. In a time before cell phones, I couldn't call them and say, *"I changed my mind."* (That was a good thing. You'll see why later.) I immediately called my older sister, Kathy (who was back at home), from a payphone and cried to her. What a blessing she was to me, comforting me at that time.

That night in my dorm room, I went to bed early and cried and cried as I had never cried before. I begged God for help but couldn't feel Him anywhere. I thought He didn't care. Little did I know that He did care and was about to send help in a big way. Someone knocked on my door and a few people I had just met earlier that day asked if I wanted to go out with them. I didn't go since I wasn't ready, but I felt great relief like someone did care and that everything would be OK. I didn't fully realize it at the time, but they were the answer to my prayer I so desperately prayed to God. I asked Him for help, and He sent me friends. I would go on to spend a lot of time with those amazing friends.

I wish I could say that I went to church to seek God's comfort and support over the next few weeks and months, but I didn't. I had distanced myself from God when I was in college in Hays, Kansas, and pretty much only talked to Him when I needed help or wanted something. I was also kind of angry with God since I thought He had deserted me when my family left, and I felt lonely. I didn't see that He HAD sent me help, just not in the way I was expecting. (I thought the pain and loneliness from missing my family would magically go away.) How much suffering would have been alleviated if I would have turned to my Heavenly Father and Mother Mary to comfort me? God was looking out for me though and was there even though I didn't feel Him.

"I waited patiently for the Lord; He inclined to me and heard my cry. He drew me up from the desolate pit, out of the miry bog, and set my feet upon a rock, making my steps secure. He put a new song in my mouth, a song of praise to our God." Psalm 40:1-3

Reflection

Have you ever felt your heart was broken? Did you turn to God in that time? In experiencing that, how are you better able to help others who go through heartache?

Day 6

Forgiveness

"Have mercy on me, O God, according to Thy steadfast love; according to Thy abundant mercy blot out my transgressions. Wash me thoroughly from my iniquity, and cleanse me from my sin."
Psalms 51:1-2

Unfortunately, during my college years, I turned my back on God. I didn't realize I had done it; it had happened a little at a time. I missed Mass one week, then another. I became a "Christmas and Easter Catholic." I went out and partied with my friends and did things I shouldn't have done. I was pretty much looking out for myself. I disobeyed God's laws, but still asked Him for help when I needed it. Yes, I was very selfish and self-centered. I hate to think of what could have happened if I had died in my sins. I wish I could erase those years or go back and act like a Christian, but all I could do was offer my sorrow, ask forgiveness, and be thankful that God was looking out for me. God was very patient with me during those years. He still loved me in spite of all my sins and the pain that I caused.

I was a lost sheep, waiting to be found.

"What man of you, having a hundred sheep, if he has lost one of them, does not leave the ninety-nine in the wilderness, and go after the one which is lost, until he finds it? And when he has found it, he lays it on his shoulders, rejoicing." Luke 15:3-4

One year for Christmas, my mom and dad gave me the movie of the story of Fatima. I was just amazed that Mary had appeared to the three children in Fatima and I hadn't even heard about it. It touched me deeply. Over the next few months, I started to develop a relationship with Mary who brought me to Jesus. During this time, I also met Mike and got married. Getting married in the church drew me closer to the faith. Not long after that, I would be touched by the reality of Jesus in the Blessed Eucharist and He would change my life forever. Just as it happens with so many fallen-away Catholics, Mary brought me to Jesus.

"Just so, I tell you, there will be more joy in heaven over one sinner who repents than over ninety-nine righteous persons who need no repentance." Luke 15:7

Reflection

God has forgiven us countless times. Every time we ask for forgiveness, He is ready to forgive and heal us.

As God has forgiven us, we are called to forgive others. In fact, when we pray the Lord's Prayer, we find that we will be forgiven WHEN we forgive others. *"And forgive us our trespasses AS WE FORGIVE those who trespass against us."*

Is there anyone you still need to forgive?

If you are having trouble forgiving someone who has hurt you, pray for God to help you. I suggest reading *"Left to Tell"* by Immaculee Ilibagiza. Immaculee was able to forgive the Hutus in Rwanda for killing her family, friends, neighbors, and over one million of her people, the Tutsis, in the Rwandan Genocide of 1994. Her story of forgiveness is a beautiful example of the transformation that is possible when one is open to God's grace.

- Faith step: It is a good practice to go to confession once a month. Even if you don't have mortal sin, it helps you to see how the little things you do keep you from growing in grace. It also helps to have the same priest as a spiritual advisor to help you know how to overcome certain sins.

Day 7

This Roller Coaster Ride Called 'Marriage'

"For this reason a man shall leave his father and mother and be joined to his wife, and the two shall become one. This is a great mystery, and I mean in reference to Christ and the church; however, let each one of you love his wife as himself, and let the wife see that she respects her husband."

Ephesians 5:31-33

One night as my college friend Debbie and I were getting ready to go out to the dance club, I didn't feel like going. I tried to talk her out of going and instead, she talked me into it. Little did I know, I would have her to thank for changing the course of my life.

When we got to the club, it was already busy, so we had to stand instead of sit, much to my dismay. God works in mysterious ways though, bringing people together who were meant to be together. Mike noticed me, the "tall girl," and my friend from across the room and came over and asked me to dance. His friend also found my friend and we danced and talked the night away.

On our second date, he came to pick me up and brought me over to an old pickup truck. I didn't think anything of it, but he laughed and said, *"No, this is my car."* His car was a really nice Ford Escort. When he put on his "driving gloves," I thought, *"Oh my gosh, I should have listened to my mom. He is like a murderer or something."* Well, thankfully he wasn't. We got to the pizza place and sat down. The booth behind us had a family with a couple of children and Mike played peek-a-boo with the little boy as we waited for our pizza. He didn't know it, but right then, Mike stole my heart. I knew if he liked kids that much, he was special. (We would go on to have 13 of our own. I joke with him saying if he would have known that at the time, he would have run away screaming.)

As I got to know Mike over the next few weeks, I knew he was much different than other guys I had dated. I couldn't put my finger on it but I knew there was something special about him. When we were together, I didn't want to be apart from him. He made me laugh. He was cute. He was fun. He was kind of a jokester. He had many of the same beliefs I had. He was considerate.

We had only been dating three months when he flew to Kansas with me to make sure my family wasn't weird. On the flight home, he pulled out a ring and asked me to marry him. I was totally shocked. I really didn't see it coming. First, I wondered if the ring was real, or if he was just joking around with me. Yep, it was real. I gave him the response he was hoping for, *"Yes!"* A bit later, a flight attendant approached us and asked us if we just got engaged and we joyfully told her yes. As the flight landed, she congratulated us over the loudspeaker, and everyone clapped. (I wouldn't recommend for someone to get engaged only three months after they meet, but for us, it worked.)

Over the years, life with Mike has been like a roller coaster ride. Just as we were at a high point in our marriage, something would happen, and we would come crashing down. Life with Mike has been wonderful, amazing, fun, and difficult. We both have our weaknesses, sins, and faults, and we forgive each other seven times 70 times, as Jesus asks us to. Mike has been there supporting me in the most difficult times of my life. He has been there with me sharing the happiest times of my life. I can't imagine going on this journey with anyone else.

Heaven touched earth on that fateful night when we met. In a SoCal metro area of millions of people, we went to the same dance club on the same night and somehow found each other.

"This is my commandment, that you love one another as I have loved you." John 15:12

Reflection

What roller coaster rides has God called you on in your life? Are you on a marriage roller coaster? Single life? Consecrated life? How have you handled the ups and downs?

Day 8

Being Set Free

"...If you continue in my word, you are truly my disciples, and you will know the truth, and the truth will make you free."

John 8:31-32

As we draw closer to God, open up to Him, and let Him in every aspect of our lives, He is able to bring to the forefront of our minds the incidents or people who have hurt us in the past. He can then go in, heal those moments, and heal our hearts and lives. It is very difficult to open memories that have been suppressed, sometimes for decades. It is very difficult to bring back those memories that have deeply hurt us, but in doing so, God can heal our hearts and let us see those memories through HIS eyes. God can redeem and re-write our memories through His eyes.

Some people have horrible, horrible memories to overcome and my heart breaks for the pain which so many people have gone through. I have no horrible memories, just some regular bad memories. God can heal every memory, every pain, no matter how big or how small. Heaven touches earth when we allow God to set us free from bad experiences.

"Look at the giraffe." (laughter)

Yes, that's me. I was (am) the giraffe. At 5'10" tall in middle school, wearing high heels, and super skinny with no figure, I suppose that is what I looked like.

I had been in a great mood. We had just finished a music festival at our small-town school, and we got to sing and learn new things. It had been a lot of fun. Why did these kids from some other town have to ruin it?

My first thought when ridiculed was, *"Just wait, I'm going to grow up and become a beautiful model. Then you won't be laughing."*

Sadly, that happening (even though it got pushed to the back of my mind) became kind of my mindset after that. *"If I am not beautiful, I am not worthy,"* were my thoughts after that incident.

As I went through high school and college, I did get prettier and fill out a little. I didn't become the supermodel I'd envisioned, but it felt good not being the ugly duckling. I was finally a swan (of sorts).

(Just for the record, I always thought the ugly duckling was cuter than the swan.)

After I married and started having children, any memory of that day in middle school was buried. I was in motherhood-survival-mode, operating on a few hours of sleep each night taking care of my children. That day only resurfaced as I woke up in middle age. My looks were fading. My life was changing. The memory of that day was hurting me once again.

So, I revisit that day in my mind to redeem it, to get my self-esteem back. I am the same young girl. It happens the same. It is a cold, yet sunny day. I walk outside. The middle school kids are there. The name-calling and laughter still happen. And yet, it is different.

Jesus is there. I feel Jesus beside me, looking at THEM in sorrow.

"You are MY little giraffe," Jesus says to me with kindness and love. Gazing into the eyes of Jesus, I can see a glimpse of His great love for me as he looks at me with compassion. Somehow, the degrading comment of the kids turns into a term of endearment when used by Jesus. The bad feelings evaporate into the air as tears fill my eyes. It is just Jesus and me and He is looking at me with love in his eyes.

After that, I only feel sorrow for the kids of my younger years. I am sorry that they felt the need to put someone else down in order to build themselves up. I hope the rest of their lives turned out better than that very low moment. I pray they have found God.

I forgive them.

I am set free.

Reflection

While those kids in middle school crushed my spirit that day, many other people I met during my life used uplifting words instead of tearing down words. I remember the kind words of two older ladies who came into the restaurant I worked at. I was a freshman in high school and was still at an awkward stage in my young life. As I served them one night, one of them said to the other, *"Tall people are so graceful and elegant."* I laughed and said, *"Not me, I'm clumsy and awkward."* She gently told me, *"No, you are graceful too."*

I never forgot those kind words.

We have the power to use words that lift others up or crush their spirits. How can we lift others up today?

What memories do you need to be redeemed and re-written?

Revisit those times with Jesus and allow Him to set you free.

Day 9

God's Presence in Sorrow

"Is there anyone among you suffering? Let him pray. Is any cheerful? Let him sing praise." James 5:13

Before I got pregnant with Amber, our first child, I came to the realization that, although many Catholics use birth control, something didn't seem right about it. I went to a priest who told me it was a personal decision and to follow my conscience. I thought, *"Follow my conscience, what kind of answer is that from a priest?"* I wanted to know if it was right or wrong. I followed my conscience and stopped using birth control.

In the months to follow, I found out that the church teaches that artificial contraception is wrong. *"But why was it considered wrong?"* I wondered. After more searching (especially reading Humanae Vitae, the 1968 encyclical of Pope Paul VI), I learned that the marital act of union must always

be unitive and procreative or open to life. Did that mean we were supposed to have as many children as we possibly could? No, it didn't. (This is a teaching of the church that is often misunderstood by people who just assume things and don't do enough research.) It took much prayer and study for me to finally understand this teaching. I discovered that the *Creighton Method of Natural Family Planning* based on NaPro Technology is the natural means in which we can work with God to conceive children or postpone pregnancy for good reasons. The *Creighton Method* is very accurate and safe (contrary to artificial birth control which can cause strokes and some of which can cause abortion). The *Creighton Method* is natural and 97-99% effective when used to postpone pregnancy. It does take commitment and self-control.
To find out more, go to:
https://www.naprotechnology.com/or
https://www.creightonmodel.com

After Amber was born, we wanted another child. I got pregnant but knew something was wrong. I kept bleeding and it wouldn't stop, even with bed rest. Mike took me to the emergency room, and we were told that I had miscarried the baby. The doctor let me know that he had to do a D & C. I was heartbroken and very scared. Mike couldn't be in the room with me so I prayed during the procedure that Jesus would be there to hold my hand. Heaven touched earth then because I felt a sense of peace descend on me like a warm blanket. I felt Jesus holding my hand and knew everything would be OK. My baby was with Jesus.

Since that time, we have named the baby and three other

babies who we lost in miscarriage. We pray to ask them to intercede before God to help us. We have a spiritual connection with Amy Agnes, Abby Esther, John Michael, and Anthony John Paul. They are our family just as much as the children who are living on earth. We will never meet our babies on earth, but we will be with them in heaven.

Reflection

Can you remember a sorrowful time in your life when you felt the presence of God with you? What did you learn from it? The next time you go through a sorrowful time, it is a good practice to praise and worship God, even in the sorrow.

"I will bless the Lord at all times; His praise shall continually be in my mouth." Psalm 34:1

Day 10

Be Thankful for the "No"

"For my thoughts are not your thoughts, neither are your ways my ways, says the Lord. For as the heavens are higher than the earth, so are my ways higher than your ways and my thoughts than your thoughts." Isaiah 55:8-9

Our priest one day told us to be thankful for the prayers that God answers with a *"No."* There is a reason that He says no. Later, I thought about what he said and thought about my own life.

When I was in college in Kansas, I wanted a Volkswagen Rabbit Convertible. It was such a cute car and I wanted it so badly. My mom reminded me of the car payments I would have when my income was already so small. I didn't get the car and was very disappointed. However, looking back, all I can say is, *"Thank You, Jesus!"* If I'd had those car payments, I would not have been able to afford to move to California.

I would not have met Mike and had my 13 amazing kids. Wow! A big thank you to God! Sometimes heaven touches earth by God telling us, *"No!"* Who knew?

Years later, when I was in my late 20's and married with one child, our Lord said no and no again. How? You see, I got pregnant the second and third times and I lost both babies in miscarriage, one right after the other. I was totally devastated. *"Why was this happening?"* I tearfully challenged God. When I finally got pregnant again, the space between Amber and the next child was four years, a lot greater than "I" had planned. But thankfully, God had different plans and little Emmalee Marie was born. Emmalee was such a blessing in all her silliness and goofiness, in her putting everything into a song, in her caring for her brothers and sisters as she got older, in her faith in God, and so many other ways.

I realized if I hadn't lost those two babies, Emmalee would never have even been conceived. As much as I wish I could have met our lost babies, I will get to meet them in heaven someday. If I hadn't had the miscarriages, I would have never met Emmalee. She just wouldn't "be."

God said no again when I lost another baby in miscarriage after Erik was born. But once again, the Lord had a plan. Sweet Kimberly Anne was born. Kimmie was such a blessing in her kind and loving nature. She was calm and peaceful with a smile that came from her heart and she touched everyone she met.

Years later, I heard that the babies born after miscarriage are called "rainbow babies," because a rainbow always appears after a storm.

Reflection

What *"No"* from God are you thankful for? How do you think your life would be different if He had said, *"Yes"*?

Day 11

Experiencing God Through Children

"...Let the children come to Me, and do not hinder them; for to such belongs the kingdom of God. Truly I say to you, whoever does not receive the kingdom of God like a child shall not enter it."
Luke 18:16

When I was younger, I knew I was an impatient person, so I prayed to God for patience. Of course, I was expecting God to suddenly and drastically change me into a patient person. In my mind, it went something like this, *"Voila, one patient person, coming up!"* Well, I soon discovered that God doesn't work like a magical genie. No, instead of making me instantaneously patient, God gave me something infinitely better. He gave me many, many opportunities to practice patience by placing in my care 13 children. Be careful what you pray for!

I must say, many of my encounters with heaven have been

through the eyes of my children. There is nothing so sweet as to hear the name of Jesus said for the first time by a little 1-year-old child. It must be the sweetest music of all to God. Seeing small children try to make the sign of the cross, genuflect in church, or run back to dip their hand in holy water for the fifth time is priceless.

I had the blessing of homeschooling my children and being with them 24/7 as they grew up. A few of them were homeschooled all through high school. The last three children were only homeschooled for a few years.

The blessings of homeschooling were great. I had the privilege of teaching every single one of my children to read. I got to teach them about the great saints, our friends in heaven. Our family did all kinds of fun things together. We took field trips and got to take vacations whenever we wanted, thus avoiding the crowds. We even got to go into a studio and record a CD of the songs and rhymes from a book I wrote. The kids sounded so cute!

Below are some heavenly experiences I had seeing my own children relate to God, family, life, and heavenly things:

One time I was in a hurry and told little 3-year-old Amber to say prayers alone that night. I left the room and out of curiosity listened at the door for a few seconds. I heard this little sweetheart saying her prayers.

Emmalee was such a goofball. She always had us laughing. She had a big heart for animals and loved those animals and insects (sometimes loving the poor little insects to death). She loved to turn everything into a song. She and Amber would sometimes have fun playing with their guardian angels.

When Erik was a baby, he would laugh at the craziest

things. We would hit a flyswatter on the countertop, and he would laugh and laugh like crazy. As a boy, he liked playing priest. He would sometimes listen to his sisters' confessions. (I guess they were OK with that.)

Kimmie has always been very sensitive and loving to others. One time, when she was 5 or 6, we were at the Catholic Center at the Citadel to talk to the priest and Kimmie saw a man in the army. She asked if she could give him a hug, and I said yes, so she went up and hugged him. He spoke with her and then came over to me and said, *"I just wanted you to know that she really made my day."*

Nicole was super brave. She was never afraid of going on roller coasters or doing scary things. She was often very serious as a baby but had a sweet smile a lot of the time as she got older to make up for it. Many times, when Kimmie, Nicole, and Ali were little and got a dollar to spend, we would go to the dollar store and they would buy something that had more than one item in it so they could share with their sisters. It was so sweet to see their generosity and helped me to forget all the arguing and fighting they did!

Ali had a little nativity set that her godmother, Kathy, gave her. She absolutely loved playing with that set. Ali would also say some very wise things as a child. I was often surprised at the wisdom coming from someone so small.

When Maria was 12, I gave her the choice of whether to be homeschooled or go to Divine Redeemer Catholic School. I told her to pray about it and God would let her know what would be best for her. She prayed and felt God calling her to go to Divine Redeemer. She was nervous about being the new kid in middle school, but I was super proud of her for doing the more difficult thing because she knew it was God's will.

Luke was our little miracle baby. The full story about him is listed later. As a little boy, he had such a joyous laugh. He always got us laughing.

Eva was, and is, the most outgoing of everyone! When Eva was 8, she was a reader at the school Mass. It was a long reading and she surprised the whole church when she said the whole reading from memory. She had memorized the whole thing!

Heaven touches earth in the precious children we have been given. They give us little glimpses of heaven each day. When I think of the great love I have for each of my children and realize that my love for them is just a fraction of God's love for each one of us, I am overwhelmed.

Reflection

"Behold, sons are a heritage from the Lord, the fruit of the womb a reward. Like arrows in the hand of a warrior are the sons of one's youth. Happy is the man who has his quiver full of them!"

Psalm 127:3-5

When have you experienced God through children? How did they touch you? How are you child-like in your own life?

Day 12

The Cry of the Poor

"...for I was hungry and you gave me food, I was thirsty and you gave me drink, I was a stranger and you welcomed me, I was naked and you clothed me, I was sick and you visited me, I was in prison and you came to me."

Matthew 25:35-36

Heaven touches earth when we see God in the poor, the sick, the suffering, the elderly, the lonely, and those who are cast out.

When I was in my 30's, with four little children, I felt a call to do volunteer work. I felt that I needed to do something with the kids, not alone. I found Silver Key and we started to deliver groceries to seniors who were homebound or didn't have transportation to pick the groceries up on their own. We met many wonderful seniors. Most of them loved seeing and visiting with the children. We received so many blessings from them.

Of course, it wasn't all happy, fun times. The older kids

probably remember my impatience in delivering the groceries. Before the time of GPS, I had to use a map and in parts of our city, it was easy to get lost, as some streets just end and pick up a few blocks later. I prayed to St. Anthony a LOT. I'm afraid I wasn't always a good example of patience and many times I just wanted to go home. It was totally worth it though. We have many good memories of elderly friends.

Many, many years later, I was in the van just going home from a fast food place. My van was stopped at the exit and I was waiting to get onto a busy street when suddenly, a homeless couple ran across the street in front of me. I had to wait for them, and as a result, I missed the chance to get into traffic. God had a plan though. The man waved at me to thank me for letting them go. Then he started to walk away but turned back to me. I rolled down my window to see what he wanted. They were obviously very cold. It was a cold and windy day, the kind of wind that puts a chill in your bones, even being outside for only a couple of minutes. He told me they didn't have a place to stay and asked for help. I didn't have any cash, so I told him about the soup kitchen and told him there were shelters. He said they had stayed in a shelter before, but he was uncomfortable there. I felt bad for them but didn't want to bring them home. They were total strangers. Something in my heart told me these people were alright. They really needed help and I didn't know what to do. I prayed, *"Help me!"* to God in my mind. I let them in the van and took them to a hotel and paid for one night.

"Bear one another's burdens, and so fulfil the law of Christ."

Galatians 6:2

I don't tell this story to toot my own horn or to say, *"Look at the good deed I did."* In fact, for every good deed I have done, there are many more that I should have done and didn't when God was calling me to. I share this because this couple blessed me as much or more than I blessed them. Their thankfulness was great, and I felt happy doing what God called me to do at that moment. They also made me think more about the poor and what I can do to help. The answer isn't easy as there are different reasons people are poor and homeless, and I am still searching for answers.

Jesus is truly in the poor. He was once poor.

Jesus is truly in the suffering. He suffered as none of us ever will.

Jesus is in the lonely. His loneliness, feeling the emotional impact of all our sins in the Garden of Gethsemane, was so intense, He perspired in blood.

Heaven touches earth in the poor, the sick, the elderly, the lonely. The poor are here for us to care for and love. Let us do that. How can we help the poor today?

"Now the company of those who believed were of one heart and soul, and no one said that any of the things which he possessed was his own, but they had everything in common. And with great power the apostles gave their testimony to the resurrection of the Lord Jesus, and great grace was upon them all. There was not a needy person among them, for as many as were possessors of lands or houses sold them, and brought the proceeds of what was sold

and laid it at the apostles' feet; and distribution was made to each as any had need." Acts 4:32-35

Reflection

Have you had an experience with the poor, the sick, the elderly, or the lonely that touched your heart? What did you learn?

- Faith step: How can you serve the poor and outcast?

"If you pour yourself out for the hungry and satisfy the desire of the afflicted, then shall your light rise in the darkness and your gloom be as the noonday." Isaiah 58:10

Day 13

A Surprise Visit from Jesus

"Truly, truly, I say to you, unless you eat the flesh of the Son of man and drink his blood, you have no life in you; he who eats my flesh and drinks my blood has eternal life, and I will raise him up at the last day. For my flesh is food indeed and my blood is drink indeed. He who eats my flesh and drinks my blood abides in me, and I in him." John 6:53-56

When I went into the hospital to give birth to our seventh child, I was very nervous, as I always was when giving birth, about the pain that lay ahead. As I was lying there in labor, a woman came in and asked if I would like to receive Jesus in the Blessed Eucharist. I cannot even put into words how ecstatic I was. I was overwhelmed with joy that Jesus would come to me when I needed Him most.

As I got ready to receive Our Lord, the thought crossed my mind that Jesus was preparing me for something difficult in my labor. I first thought of more pain or even a C-section. Then my thoughts went to our preborn child. What if Jesus wanted to take her to heaven? I prayed that God wasn't asking me to give her up.

When I finally received Our Lord in Communion, I was filled with a great sense of peace and joy. God was there with me, helping me, loving me, giving me strength. I knew that whatever God asked of me, I could do.

Shortly after I received Jesus, the pushing pains began, and I was ready to give birth. I discovered that the epidural they had given me for pain was only working on a certain area of my body and once the baby started moving down the birth canal, the pain was overwhelming. Thankfully the delivery did not last long and while the pain was very intense, it was short. Our dear baby, Maria Clare, was born. As I held her in my arms, so proud and thankful for such a beautiful child, I was also in a state of happiness and peace because of the love Jesus had given to me.

As Catholics, we are able to receive the Blessed Eucharist every day if we wish! We are so very blessed! I pray that everyone comes to the realization of Jesus' presence in the Eucharist. This is the heart of our faith. It is Jesus in the Blessed Eucharist that sustains me.

"I am the living bread which came down from heaven; if anyone eats of this bread, he will live forever; and the bread which I shall give for the life of the world is my flesh." John 6:50-51

Reflection

How has Jesus surprised you with graces in your life? Do you spend time with Him in Adoration?

- Faith step: Why not spend an hour with Jesus this week? If you can't do an hour, start with ½ hour. In our crazy, noisy, chaotic world, we NEED times of silence. We need peace.

It's God I See

I look up in the Monstrance,
Who is there for me?
My heart does not deceive me,
For it is God I see.

God the Father,
God the Son,
God the Spirit,
Three in One.

God majestic,
God in glory,
God is hidden,
This is His story.

He is always waiting here,
Whenever I may need Him.
I wish that I could stay here always,
And forever see Him.

Day 14

God's Voice

"My son, be attentive to my words; incline your ear to my sayings. Let them not escape from your sight; keep them within your heart. For they are life to him who finds them and healing to all his flesh." Proverbs 4:20-21

Heaven touches earth when we hear God's voice or feel in our hearts that He is telling us something or leading us down a certain path. I remember one time I heard God speak to my heart when I was pregnant with Maria. I was hoping she would be a boy so Erik would have a brother. I was at Eucharistic Adoration and I asked God if the baby was a boy. I felt Him say, *"You will have a boy, but you will have to suffer."* Of course, when Maria was born and was a girl, I discounted that the message was from God. It was only after I gave birth to Luke and he went through all of his medical troubles that I remembered what God had said.

"How does God speak to me?" I often wondered that when I was younger. I thought it was so difficult to hear God's voice.

What did He sound like? How did I know if a thought was from God? It was only through prayer and silence that I have discovered that God speaks to me (and all of us) in so, so many ways. To hear His voice, I just need to be silent and be aware of Him in my presence. As I draw closer to God, it becomes clearer when and how He is speaking to me. I learn to recognize the voice of my loving Father, even though I can't see Him. Here are just a few examples:

God may speak to us in a gentle breeze on a warm day. He speaks directly to our hearts and says, *"I love you,"* in that gentle breeze.

God speaks to us through the people around us, through the care and kindness of those we love, through the smile of a stranger, through the advice or support of a friend. He speaks to us in the unconditional love of a child.

God speaks to us through His Word in the Bible. He gives us comfort through the Word. He gives us joy, inspiration, and a guide which we need for life.

God sometimes speaks directly to our hearts, giving us an inspiration or letting us feel His love. He speaks to our minds, placing in our consciousness holy thoughts and ideas.

God speaks to us in our suffering, uniting Himself with us, even when we don't feel His presence.

God sometimes speaks to us in dates and numbers. Was it a coincidence that St. John Paul died on the vigil of Divine Mercy Sunday, which was also the first Saturday? No. Was it a coincidence that my dad died on a Good Friday? No.

God sometimes speaks to us in dates and numbers.

We find the voice of God, not amidst the noise of our world, but in the silence.

"Before you speak, it is necessary for you to listen, for God speaks in the silence of the heart." St. Teresa of Calcutta

Reflection

Sometimes it is hard to discern the voices in our lives that pop into our heads, or the action we may feel God calling us to engage in, but we get better with practice. It is a lifelong effort, discerning if the voice we hear is just coming from us, from God, or from the devil. A spiritual director can help us in this discerning process.

In what ways have you heard God's voice in your own life? How often do you spend time being still and listening to God?

- Faith step: Discover your own daily encounters with God. Look for signs from God during your day. Take quiet times during the day just to listen to Him.
- If you enjoy writing, write down what you feel or what you think God is telling you. No matter how wonderful they seem, you will forget many of the experiences you have if you don't record or write them down in some way. If you write them down, you can look back and see how God was working in your life at a certain time or what He was saying to you. Sometimes you don't discover the meaning until years later. You'll be pleasantly surprised when

you see God or hear Him speaking to you in the seemingly minute parts of your life. It is a joy to discover the ways in which God is speaking. In this way, your whole day can be turned into a prayer and your relationship with God will grow.

Day 15

A Special Surprise

"Every good endowment and every perfect gift is from above, coming down from the Father of lights with whom there is no variation or shadow due to change." James 1:17

When I moved to California at the age of 21, it was my dream to someday work for Walt Disney Studios. (This was back in the days when Disney made good movies and everything they made was family-friendly. Unfortunately, those times are now gone. They have taken a horrible turn in the last couple of decades.) I knew I was a very mediocre artist, but I had a great imagination and felt like my imagination would open doors that my lack of talent would slam shut.

I admired Walt Disney and how he had created Disneyland to be the "Happiest Place on Earth." I loved the story he told of how when he was a young father, he would take his two girls to the carnival to watch them ride the rides. As he sat on the bench watching them, he thought of how great it would be if families could have the whole carnival experience together, adults and children riding the rides together.

He wanted to make a magical place for all and for families to be brought closer together at Disneyland.

"The important thing is the family. If you can keep the family together—and that's the backbone of our whole business, catering to families—that's what we hope to do." Walt Disney

In May of 2006, our family took a vacation to Disneyland. We knew it would probably be our last trip since it was so expensive for a family with eight children (Number 8, Luke, was still preborn). Also, Mike's mom, who we always stayed with, was moving to Texas, which would mean another trip would cost us gas money to get there, money for tickets, food, AND a place to stay, just too much money for a large family living on one income.

We were shocked and surprised when Emmalee was greeted as the honorary 2 billionth guest to visit a Disney theme park. As Emmalee walked through the gates into Disneyland, hundreds of streamers shot up into the air, the band played, and the princesses and Disney characters were there to greet her, along with the mayor of Disneyland.

The whole Disney cast welcomed Emmalee. They took pictures and did interviews. Emmalee and the whole family (as well as my sister Kathy, her daughter, Megan, and Mike's mom, who came too) were treated like royalty that day. We had a personal escort all day, which meant no waiting in line for rides! Emmalee and some of the family even got to ride the Matterhorn with Mickey Mouse. We received free meals, which were amazing, and got to visit the princesses at a special lunch. (The little girls, Kimmie, Nicole, Ali, and Maria, ages 8, 6, 4, and 2 at the time, were in heaven!) They gave us all golden Mickey Mouse ears with our names on them for Disneyland's 50th anniversary (even baby Luke who wasn't born yet), and the Disney photographer took many pictures. Emmalee also got to be the grand marshall of the Disney parade and she, and the whole family got to ride in Walt Disney's very own fire engine and be in the parade. We got to stay in the grand suite of the Disney hotel, and best of all, Emmalee received a lifetime silver pass for her and nine guests (they based it on the size of our family, including Luke), to get into any Disney park for free, for life!

I pondered these happenings a lot as the months went by. Did God have a hand in this? I think God smiled on us that day. It just so happened that we chose May to go to California and it so happened that we chose the very day the 2 billionth person would visit a Disney park. (They didn't know who the EXACT 2 billionth person would be, they just knew it would happen around that day, so they chose someone they deemed worthy.) It just so happened that we were in the right line. (I would have chosen the line away from the cameras, but Mike was curious and got in line first.) It just so happened that Mike was wearing his Home Makeover shirt. (The company Mike worked for sponsored a home that was built for a needy family.) A Disney official noticed Mike's shirt and chatted with him about it while we waited in line. I believe that had something to do with their decision.

I like to think God gave our angels the go-ahead to give a little nudge to those in charge, who then noticed Emmalee, the perfect age (12) to appreciate and receive such a gift.

Perhaps God wanted this to happen to make people notice that there are still large families around. Perhaps it happened so people would recognize the preborn (since preborn baby Luke was included in the lifetime pass, and it was noted on T.V. and in all the newspapers). Perhaps it was a gift to us for following the will of God, for being open to having a large family. I can guess and guess why it happened, but ultimately, I don't know. I'm just glad it did happen. It was a great gift. One day in heaven, we will know the big picture.

Reflection

It is comforting to me to know that God never forgets our dreams. My heavenly Father knew how much I loved the magical world of Disney and he knew that when I was younger, I had given up on my dream to work for Disney to get married and have a family. Although my dream to work for Walt Disney Studios didn't come true, God had a much greater dream and gift for me in my husband and all of my children.

Even in all this, even with all the gifts God had already given me, He didn't forget my original dream and love of Disney. He gave my whole family, especially Emmalee, an amazing surprise.

What dreams have you had in your life? Did they come true? If not, did God transform them into something even greater?

Day 16

Life Lessons from a Preborn Child

"Thou hast turned for me my mourning into dancing; Thou hast loosed my sackcloth and girded me with gladness, that my soul may praise Thee and not be silent. O Lord my God, I will give thanks to Thee forever." Psalm 30:11-13

When I look back at what we went through with our preborn child Luke, I see that the hand of God was everywhere.

In that darkened ultrasound room, at seven months pregnant, I was told that Luke had CCAM, Congenital Cystic Adenomatoid Malformation, or cysts in one of his lungs. This was a serious condition. The doctor told me that Luke may survive birth, or he might die when he was born. I called my husband in tears. This was devastating.

Those final two months of pregnancy were very difficult, not physically, but emotionally. Seeing mothers with newborn babies put me into depression, knowing that my Luke might not survive.

As a mother who had given birth seven times previously, my focus on my preborn babies had always been, *"Hurry up and grow so you can be born."* With Luke it was different. I wanted Luke to stay in the womb, where I knew he was in the safest place he would ever be. I began to cherish the life inside of me more than I had ever done before, knowing it may be the only time I had with Luke. I discovered, even with all the aches and pains, that pregnancy was a joy. I took special time to let my other children come up and touch my belly and watch baby Luke do all sorts of contortions and movements. Little Maria, even before this was all discovered, would come up to my belly, lift up my shirt, and say, *"Hi baby Duke! Come out, baby Duke!"*

This difficult time was also a blessing in disguise in another way, for God worked on the hearts of our family members and developed in us a deep love for preborn children that we had only had a glimpse of before. We discovered how precious life was on a whole new level since we were experiencing how it could be gone in a heartbeat. We knew God had a purpose for every single life. We knew that even if Luke did not live past the first few days, hours, or minutes, he was put on earth for a reason.

Throughout this ordeal, I saw the hand of God in all of our friends and family around us. It was as if God was placing us in a cocoon of love and support. So many people were praying for baby Luke. I would tell one person and they would tell everyone they knew. I saw the work of the church as one, the church militant fighting for one of its own. Little notes and prayer cards that were sent helped to lift my spirit. (Never underestimate the power of simple words of encouragement.)

I have had a devotion to Our Lady of Guadalupe since I was younger. Our family began saying a novena to Our Lady of Guadalupe, putting everything in Mary's hands. Mary knew the joy of having a healthy Son and she also knew the sorrow of losing her Son, so I knew she would be with us no matter what happened. We offered our suffering and Luke's suffering for the preborn and for a friend who was in trouble. We also prayed to St. Luke, his namesake, St. Michael, and to Luke's guardian angel.

Another blessing was given to us when we discovered they wouldn't deliver Luke here in Colorado Springs, but in Denver where they had a heart/lung bypass machine called ECMO. The name of the hospital? St. Luke's of course! Another little gift from God in the midst of a crisis.

We were praying for a miracle and were hoping for the best, but we wanted to do God's will and would accept what His plan was. We realized that He could see the big picture that we couldn't see; we realized that He knew what was best for us all.

When Luke was born at St. Luke's in Denver, the staff was ready for the worst. How would they save this child who may not be able to breathe, whose lungs may not function properly? On August 9, 2006, Luke was born. As he let out a strong cry, we cried with him. Luke's cry was the most beautiful sound I had ever heard before or have heard since. The medical staff rushed Luke to NICU, put him in an oxygen tent, and monitored him very closely. Luke had surgery the next morning, at one day old, to remove 2/3 of his right lung. In surgery, the laparoscopic equipment malfunctioned resulting in massive blood loss. The surgeon had to do CPR to revive our little baby. Praise be to God that Luke pulled through! Luke was placed on a respirator and spent five weeks in NICU with many victories and many setbacks before he could come home on oxygen. Luke went through many difficult times in his early years, but he is now 13 years old and is a healthy, kind, and energetic boy.

Luke's right lung has grown back.

A few months after Luke came home from the hospital, I got yet another surprise. The new church year was starting in November and it was the year of Luke! (The church reads the Gospels in the Bible in three-year cycles, A, B, and C: Matthew, Mark, and Luke. The Gospel of John is the shortest Gospel and the readings are scattered through the three-year period at the appropriate times.) I thought that this was quite wonderful that it was the Year of Luke. A celebration of life!

Heaven touched earth in the gift of Luke. Luke taught us some powerful lessons: to respect and care for the preborn, to cherish all life, and to always, always trust in God, no matter what the outcome.

"...for the Kingdom of Heaven belongs to such as these."
Matthew 19:14

Reflection

Have you learned any lessons from a preborn child? From the preborn child to a troubled teen in need of support, from a handicapped young man to an elderly grandma in her last stages, all life is precious. We are wonderfully and fearfully made!

- Faith step: How can you support the sanctity of every life, from conception to natural death?

Day 16, Part II

Stations of the Cross -- Baby Luke

These stations in no way come close to even a drop of the sufferings Jesus had. However, placing my experience in the form of the Stations of the Cross really helped me to grow closer to Jesus and unite my suffering with His, however small my sufferings were.

1. **Jesus is condemned to die.**

   When I was pregnant with Luke and they told me there were cysts in his right lung, I knew there was a good chance he would die. Jesus, it was such a small suffering compared to what You went through, but I offered it up nonetheless. It felt like a big suffering to me.
2. **Jesus takes up His cross.**

You took up Your cross and did not complain, Jesus. I carried the burden of Luke's illness and did not complain (or not much). I tried to be thankful for the time I had with him. I wasn't perfect, but I carried my cross too.

3. **Jesus falls the first time.**

   The weight of our sins, the burden of the cross, was so heavy that You fell, Jesus. I fell also, but my falling was due to my own sin and spiritual weakness.

4. **Jesus meets His mother.**

   Your mother comforted You, Jesus, as she comforted me also. She gave me courage when I needed it. She gave me hope and strength. We prayed for her intercession in the image of Our Lady of Guadalupe and she gave us comfort and hope. Thank you, Mama Mary!

5. **Simon of Cyrene helps Jesus carry the cross.**

   You sent plenty of helpers to help me carry my cross, Jesus. Before Luke's birth, we were surrounded by prayer. People would encourage us with emails, phone calls, and cards.

6. **Veronica wipes the face of Jesus.**

   Mike and I got closer during this time. He would wipe my tears and calm me. He was my strength. He was my rock. Thank you, Jesus, for giving me such a loving husband.

7. **Jesus falls a second time.**

   It was hard not to fall. I would get depressed, Jesus,

when I would see a mother and a newborn, knowing I may not have a live baby.

8. **Jesus speaks to the women of Jerusalem.**

   "Do not weep for me..." was what You said, Jesus. We offered our suffering for these women, the preborn, and a friend who was thinking about committing suicide. We wanted our suffering to go for other babies and others.

9. **Jesus falls a third time.**

   How hard it was not to despair at times, Jesus. But Your grace got us through.

10. **Jesus is stripped of His garments.**

    Just as You were stripped of Your garments, I felt stripped of the ability to do anything. It was surprisingly freeing, however, to totally depend on You.

11. **Jesus is nailed to the cross.**

    I felt somewhat nailed to the cross not knowing what to do when the time came for Luke to be born. He was to be born in a city 60 miles away and they wanted to induce labor for Luke's sake. Jesus, I prayed and prayed, and I still didn't know whether to go ahead and let them induce or wait until he came naturally. Was I not trusting You by letting them induce? Or was I not being prudent by not accepting the help that was available? We went ahead and let them induce.

12. **Jesus dies on the cross.**

    After Luke was born, we rejoiced when he could

breathe, but there were many more crosses to come. There were many times when I felt my heart die. When I saw that perfect baby on a respirator, fighting for his life, Jesus, part of me died for him right there. When we were in the hospital, my heart ached for my other children 60 miles away, but when we went home to be with them, my heart felt like it was breaking, leaving him there. When he was a few weeks old, was having trouble, and had to be put on CPAP, part of me died again.

13. **Jesus is taken down from the cross.**

    I imagine although Mary's heart was totally broken at seeing the death of her Son, a very small part of her must have felt relief that He wasn't suffering anymore. I was relieved when Luke came off the CPAP.

14. **Jesus is laid in the tomb.**

    Jesus, we got to know some parents whose little preemie babies were also in NICU. What a heartbreaking thing to go in to see Luke and notice that a baby that was there the day before was gone. We especially remember little Chloe and Jack. Why did You take them and leave Luke? Why did their parents have to suffer in such a way? I still think of them and my heart still breaks for the families who had to bury their children.

15. **Jesus rises from the dead**

    The day Luke came home from the hospital was a

day of great joy, a resurrection of sorts for our whole family. Even though he was still on oxygen, we could hold him, love him, and watch him grow and get better.

Thank you, Jesus!

Reflection

Mother Mary helped us so much in this difficult time of our lives.

When have you turned to Mary for her help in your life? She is waiting to intercede for us; she is the most loving mother we could ever have.

- Faith step: When you pray, don't forget to ask Mary to intercede. When you are afraid, ask her to enfold you in her mantle. Jesus gave us His mother for a reason. He knew she would bring us much comfort.
- Faith step: Pray the rosary every day. It is Jesus' life in Scripture in miniature.

- Faith step: Consider consecrating your family to Jesus and Mary. *"33 Days to Morning Glory"* by Michael E. Gaitley is a wonderful book of consecration that I would recommend to everyone.

Our Lady of Guadalupe, pray for us!

Day 17

Dark Nights and the Gift of the Cross

"Truly, truly, I say to you, unless a grain of wheat falls into the earth and dies, it remains alone; but if it dies, it bears much fruit. He who loves his life loses it, and he who hates his life in this world will keep it for eternal life." John 12:24-25

There are many times in life when all we feel is darkness. God seems so far away. We aren't getting any of the happy feelings that we sometimes receive when we pray. These times are so difficult. Prayer seems fruitless. We feel empty. We feel as if nothing is going right. I felt this way during my pregnancy with Luke, during the early and middle months. I would get panic attacks and feel such a feeling of hopelessness. Nothing could pull me out of this profound darkness. It was something I absolutely hated going though. It would most often happen at night when everyone else was asleep. I wondered about the darkness Jesus must have felt in the Garden of Gethsemane. My darkness was not even the most minuscule amount of the darkness Jesus experienced, so I thought about His dark night. That thought gave me some comfort, that I wasn't alone, even though I felt alone. I knew I must pray through the darkness and not desert Jesus as the disciples did in the garden.

My brief darkness was also not even a drop of what St. Mother Teresa of Calcutta experienced. Her darkness was almost lifelong, yet she remained faithful to God and the darkness was lifted at the end of her life.

"I call, I cling, I want, and there is no one to answer... Where I try to raise my thoughts to heaven, there is such convicting emptiness that those very thoughts return like sharp knives and hurt my very soul. Love—the word—it brings nothing. I am told God lives in me—and yet the reality of darkness and coldness and emptiness is so great that nothing touches my soul." St. Mother Teresa

The profound darkness St. Mother Teresa experienced is beyond my experience or understanding, but I discovered something in my own small time of darkness and suffering. I discovered that darkness in prayer is a great gift, even though it doesn't feel like it at the time. When we are not receiving consolation and happy feelings in prayer, it feels awful. We feel abandoned. However, if we persist in prayer, the fruits will be greater than we can imagine. The darkness, the dryness, is a beautiful thing because our Father, our Daddy in heaven, is calling us to His heart. He wants a deeper, more intimate relationship with us, but we honestly cannot get to that deeper relationship unless we go through the darkness first.

"There are some things in your heart that God can't do unless He takes you to a place of dryness in prayer." Fr. Mike Schmitz

During the empty periods of this time before Luke was born, God would occasionally grant me little comforts, like when I would hold a crucifix and think of what Jesus went through. It didn't make suffering easy, but it did comfort me knowing that since Jesus had suffered, He knew my suffering.

"But far be it from me to glory except in the cross of our Lord Jesus Christ, by which the world has been crucified to me, and I to the world." Galatians 6:14

The gift of the cross, the gift of salvation is the greatest gift God gave to us—Himself. Through the death of Jesus on the cross, we became sons and daughters of God. How much Jesus suffered! We cannot even begin to comprehend how much. Any other man would have died from sorrow in the garden. Jesus' love for us carried Him through the suffering all the way to the cross.

One of my favorite sayings is by St. Francis de Sales. He said,

"The everlasting God has in His wisdom foreseen from eternity, the cross He now sends you. He has considered with His all-knowing eyes, understood with His divine mind, tested with His

wise justice, warmed with loving arms and weighed with His own hands to see that it not be one ounce too heavy for you. He has blessed it with His Holy Name, anointed it with His grace, perfumed it with His consolation, and taken one last glance at you and your courage—and sent it to you from heaven, a special greeting from God to you, an alms of the all merciful love of God."

St. Francis de Sales

Reflection

What dark night have you experienced? How did you feel once the dark night was over?

St. Ignatius of Loyola taught about spiritual consolation and desolation. St. Ignatius said that when we are in desolation, even though we don't feel like praying, we should **increase** our prayer and meditation, have more examination, and more penance, even if we don't feel like it.

For more information about consolation and desolation, just look up St. Ignatius of Loyola.

Day 18

Doing the Will of God -- Blessing Multiplied

"Whoever does the will of God is my brother, and sister, and mother." Mark 3:35

I met a young lady at Mass one week and would see her from time to time. We didn't always say much to each other, but she was always a joy to see. She was always happy and friendly. I never would have guessed she was shy.

One day after Mass, she invited my oldest daughter (then 15) to a Challenge group meeting. (At the time, I had been praying for my daughter to find a way to meet other girls her own age.) The young woman later told us that it was very difficult for her to tell us about the Challenge meeting because of her shy nature. I'm sure she prayed for the courage to be able to do so. She did God's will even though it was difficult.

That one invitation led to so many blessings in our lives. My daughter, Amber, joined Challenge. My other daughter, Emmalee, joined also. They both made good Catholic and

Christian friends. Emmalee met Maggie, who would become her very best friend in high school.

If that were not enough, God also blessed my son Erik. The Conquest group started at the same church, the following year. Erik got to know Catholic boys and men who lived out their faith. Unfortunately, it didn't last long as they didn't have enough men to volunteer to keep it going.

Years later, Emmalee and Maggie would go on to lead the Challenge group and did an amazing job! Emmalee grew a lot. She overcame her shy nature and became a leader. Kimmie, Nicole, Ali, and Maria all joined Challenge when they were the right age and Kimmie also led Challenge for a few years.

From that one simple invitation, countless blessings have flowed.

Never underestimate the power of following God's will, even when it is tough!

Reflection

Sometimes it is difficult to do God's will. Our own fear of what He may ask us to do sometimes gets in the way. (I am still afraid of that at times.) I can tell you; God has asked things of me many times that I didn't want to do. However, when I have said yes to Him, the blessings have ALWAYS outweighed the sacrifice.

God will not call you to do something without giving you abundant graces to do it.

When is a time you found it difficult to do God's will?

Did you persevere and do it? What happened as a result of doing or not doing God's will?

What is God asking of you today?

Day 19

The Saints are Talking to Me!

"After this I looked, and behold, a great multitude which no man could number, from every nation, from all tribes and peoples and tongues, standing before the throne and before the Lamb, clothed in white robes, with palm branches in their hands, and crying out with a loud voice, 'Salvation belongs to our God who sits upon the throne, and to the Lamb.'" Revelation 7:9-10

A few years ago, when I was carrying a stack of saint cards, I dropped them, and they fell to the ground. I guess I picked them all up except one. I later found the Mother Seton card lying on the floor. Curious, I looked at the saint calendar we had, and lo and behold, it was Mother Seton's feast day!

Another time I found a saint card on the floor. At Mass that evening, I discovered it was the feast day of St. John Bosco. My mind traveled back to earlier in the day when, yes, the St. John Bosco card was the one on the floor. (Believe it or not, we don't make a habit of leaving saint cards on the floor.) That's cool! The saints were talking to me!

St. Anthony is in a category all his own! He has come to my aid so many times and has never let me down. When I was blessed to go to Italy in 2014, we visited St. Anthony's tomb. I cried. I love him.

My three favorite saints are St. Peter, St. John Paul the Great, and St. Joan of Arc, although I have many more favorites as well. I can identify with St. Peter as it seems he was impulsive, as I can be at times. He was also a bit stubborn, as I am as well. Seeing what Peter overcame in his own imperfections to be all that God called him to be gives me hope that I can overcome my imperfections as well.

St. John Paul was an amazing example of how to live as Christ did. I felt his love for us when I heard him speak when I was a teen. He really and truly loved God and all of us.

St. Joan of Arc is my confirmation saint. She was brave and faithful to God's call, as I can be WHEN I depend on God. I speak to her and ask for her help, especially when leading 40 Days for Life efforts.

My children all know when we sing the *"Litany of the Saints"* on All Saint's Day, I start crying or at the very least get tears in my eyes. Why? I am reminded of our heavenly brothers and sisters, all the wonderful, amazing saints, who are there with us at every Mass. I feel closest to them during that time. I can't wait to get to meet them all!

Reflection

Heaven touches earth in God's gift of the saints, our brothers, and sisters in heaven.

Call on the saints and angels to intercede for you before God every day. They wait in earnest to help us.

Who are your favorite saints? Spend some time learning more about them.

Along with the saints, we mustn't forget to call on our guardian angels for help. I have told my children to ask their guardian angels to go on missions for them. We can all do this. When we pray, in our minds, we can ask our angel to go visit a sick or dying person or someone in need. We then journey with our angel in spirit to that person to comfort them.

- Faith step: Talk to your guardian angel every day. Ask your angel to visit someone who God places on your heart today.

To "Papa"

In memory of St. John Paul the Great, 1920-2005
(Originally printed in *Fun with Bible Stories*, 2005)

We watched you when we were young,
As you became the pope.
You told us to always trust in God,
And that with Christ there was always hope.

You touched billions of lives,
In person and on T.V.
You were compassionate and kind,
And sometimes also funny.

Even over the television screen,
Compassion you portrayed.
We could see the very love of Christ,
In the actions you displayed.

You reminded us that life is precious,
Especially in the womb.
You taught us there can be dignity and value in suffering,
When one approaches the tomb.

You taught us about the sanctity of life,
You taught us to forgive.
You showed us how to help each other,
And showed us how to live.

You sometimes ruffled feathers,
In your preaching of the truth,
But you were also loved by many,
Especially the youth.

We didn't have to meet you,
To experience your love and care.
We considered you our "Papa,"
And knew you'd always be there.

But now you go to your reward,
And you're singing a happy tune.
We will hold you in our hearts forever,
And we'll see you someday soon.

Saint John Paul II, we love you!!

Day 20

God's Wonderful Sense of Humor!

"He who blesses his neighbor with a loud voice, rising early in the morning, will be counted as cursing." Proverbs 27:14

God has a wonderful sense of humor!

"Oh, no!" Some people may say. *"God is up on His cloud, running the world. He is very serious."*

I beg to differ!

He made us in His image and likeness, right?

We have a sense of humor and so does He. (I mean, read the Bible verse shared here from Proverbs. It is hilarious!) I personally can't wait to get to know more about God and His sense of humor!

I have a few examples of God's sense of humor. For instance, I should know never to say, *"I will NEVER do something."* As a child I said I would never drive a car—I did! As a teen, I said I'd never go to college—did it and graduated! As a teen, I said I'd never get married and have children—not only did it, but I have 13 children. I can picture God finding a little amusement in it all. He can change hearts in big ways. (I am a little concerned about this one as I have always said, *"I will never parachute from an airplane..."*)

One of my children has utterly tested me to the very limit of my being. More than any of my other children, she has managed to push every one of my buttons, revealing a side of me I never knew I had (not a good side, mind you). I continuously had to discipline her, mainly because of her disobedience. One day, I was at the end of my rope, literally dangling from the end from a high precipice, praying to the Holy Spirit to help me discipline her. The Holy Spirit gave me such a revelation, I felt like I was hit in the head with a brick.

"She is like you!"

"What?" "No!" "What?" I must not have heard right.

"Yes," the Holy Spirit let me know, *"she IS like you."*

"In what way?" I wanted to know.

He revealed to me that I also like to follow my own will and not listen to what everyone tells me, including my husband.

The Holy Spirit showed me that the way she rebels against me is the same way I rebel against God sometimes. Sure, it is great following God when He asks me to do something I don't mind doing. But when He asks me to do something I don't want to do, it's hard to give up my will. I know that He knows what is best for me and He knows the best paths for me to take, but to do what He wants ALL the time? Whoa! Wait a minute! That's kind of hard!

I've talked to my daughter many times and she really wants to be good. She really wants to listen and is sorry (later...sometimes...) when she is disobedient. This is just like me also. I want to be obedient to God, but my own will gets in the way sometimes.

I see God's sense of humor in the fact that He has given me a wonderful, yet very stubborn and willful child to show me one thing I need to change in myself. What a gift she is. She will help me grow in my spiritual life even if it kills me in the process!

After I wrote this, I realized that I didn't want to only include negative things about this daughter (because, trust me, when she reads this, she will know I am writing about her). This stubborn daughter is also artistic. She is highly intelligent, a deep thinker. She has a great sense of humor and always makes me laugh. She is beautiful. She has many good friends. She has a good foundation of faith. I can see her going on to do great things in her life as long as she stays rooted in her faith in God. She has been a great blessing to me in my life in so many ways and I am eternally grateful to God for her life.

Reflection

The Proverb above (Proverb 27:14) shows God's sense of humor.

In what ways have you seen God's sense of humor at work?

Day 21

A Father's Love

"My God, my God, why hast thou forsaken me? Why art thou so far from helping me, from the words of my groaning? Oh my God, I cry by day, but thou dost not answer; and by night, but find no rest." Psalm 22:1-5

When Luke, at age 2 1/2, was in the hospital with RSV (respiratory syncytial virus), I got a small glimpse of our heavenly Father's role in His love for us. You see, I had to stand there and hold Luke's hands down as the nurse stuck a suction clear up into his nose to clean it out. It looked very painful and uncomfortable. Luke, of course, squirmed and kicked and screamed to the point of looking like he was going to pass out. Toward the end of the ordeal, he yelled out, *"MOMMY!!"* which was too much for my mother's heart to handle. Here I knew that cleaning out his nose was what he needed most because afterward, he would be able to breathe better, but I couldn't make him understand that since he was too little to comprehend. My heart broke that I couldn't save him from the pain.

Afterward, I thought of how that one incident is so like our relationship with God. God will allow us to go through various pain and suffering in our lives because at that moment, that is what is best for us. God sees the final outcome which we don't see, just like a father or mother and their child. All the time, we are crying out, *"Abba," "Daddy," "Help me!"* and it seems like He's not there (just as it seemed to Luke that I wasn't there for him), but He is, holding our hands the whole time. We are just so focused on the pain; we don't see Him and we don't understand why He is letting it happen to us. We are too little to understand His ways.

Sometimes, we will not understand why He allows things this side of heaven, why He let us go through specific suffering, but sometimes we will be able to look back and see why it was allowed. I wonder, does God's heart feel as if it is going to break when He sees us going through these sufferings we go through, just like my heart felt like it was breaking when Luke was going through what he did? I'm sure it does. Jesus wept for Jerusalem. He wept for Lazarus.

When we suffer, we can think of Christ's suffering and take comfort that He is suffering with us. When we suffer, we can think of Mary's suffering and we can remember that the Father is loving us and holding our hands the whole time.

Reflection

Have you ever wondered why God allowed you to experience something traumatic or unpleasant and didn't miraculously come to your rescue?

While we may never receive an answer until we get to heaven, sometimes we do. Sometimes we see that it was allowed to protect us from something even more harmful.

Day 22

Forty Days and Beyond

"For I know the plans I have for you, says the Lord, plans for welfare and not for evil, to give you a future and a hope." Jeremiah 29:11

Many times, God calls us to carry a big cross to prepare us for something that lies ahead. I sincerely believe that going through what we did with Luke helped prepare me to lead the 40 Days for Life effort in Colorado Springs. (40 Days for Life is a nationwide effort to end abortion through prayer and fasting, vigil in front of abortion clinics, and community outreach. www.40daysforlife.com)

You see, ever since seeing *"The Silent Scream"* as a teen, I have known of the evil of abortion, but going through what we did with Luke helped me develop an appreciation of how precious and fleeting life is. Since I didn't know whether Luke would live or die when he was born, I cherished every moment that he was in utero and learned to appreciate the preborn more.

This love for the preborn was tested when I felt God calling me to lead 40 Days for Life in Colorado Springs in 2008. I prayed about taking on this task with my children and they also felt the call. I let God know the only way I could do it was if a prominent pro-life priest, Fr. Bill Carmody, would support the effort. I could not go behind his back and attempt it without his support. This wonderful priest had some misgivings when I first mentioned it, but when I called a few days later, he said, *"Let's do it!"* That was my confirmation from God.

The first 40 Days for Life in 2008 in Colorado Springs was very stressful for me. Being an introverted person, it was hard to speak in front of groups of people and call people I didn't know on the phone. I was a stay-at-home mom. I didn't have training as a speaker. I didn't have eloquent words to inspire people. And yet as has happened throughout history, God chose to work through the most unlikely person to bring glory to Himself.

"And I was with you in weakness and in much fear and trembling; and my speech and my message were not in plausible words of wisdom, but in demonstration of the Spirit and of power, that your faith might not rest in the wisdom of men but in the power of God." 1 Corinthians 2:3

During that 40 Days for Life effort, God brought together many people at the sidewalk: Catholics, Protestants, Evangelicals, Messianic Jews, and even an atheist, all there to help women and pray together. It was truly miraculous, since many of these people who didn't know each other had the same idea of opening a pregnancy center across the street from that Planned Parenthood in Old Colorado City.

After this idea was brought to the attention of Raul, the president of the local Pregnancy Center, he held a few meetings, discussing the idea of opening a new Pregnancy Center. Many people were involved, even the bishop.

A few months later, it looked like it was going to become a reality when something terrible happened and a major fundraiser which was to be held by Life Network Pregnancy Center fell through. Without the fundraiser, Life Network would not have the funds to do this. Time was running out...

As Raul called a final meeting, all of us who attended were expecting bad news. We went into the meeting, feeling very low. A Messianic Jewish pastor led us in prayer in Hebrew, which was beautiful. After the prayer, Raul spoke up. He let us know that the fundraising event had to be canceled, and so they wouldn't have the funds for a new pregnancy center. Everyone was feeling very sad, but then something miraculous happened. Raul started talking about trust in God. He spoke of the story of Gideon from the Bible. He reminded us of how Gideon had a large army to go into battle with the Midianites, but God reduced Gideon's army to only 300 men, so that in their victory, they would see that it was God's hand that would win the battle, and not the efforts of Gideon and his army. Raul shared that we were going to trust in God and take a leap of faith like Gideon.

They would open the new Pregnancy Center!

This truly was an amazing leap of faith. Raul and the board

of directors were putting the fate of the existing Pregnancy Center on the line. Why? It was because the new Pregnancy Center was clearly God's will. Raul showed us in a real way that when we trust in God and take that leap of faith, God will bless our efforts. And He did! I have never forgotten this life lesson Raul taught us. It is easy to trust in God when there is not much at stake, but when your livelihood and the livelihood of others is on the line? Can we trust then?

The new Pregnancy Center was opened across the street from the abortion clinic in Old Colorado City and many babies were saved. Planned Parenthood closed the abortion clinic 18 months after the Pregnancy Center opened. (Unfortunately, they opened another clinic on Centennial Blvd. Since then, a new Pregnancy Center has also opened ½ mile up the street from Planned Parenthood so we can be close to women in need.)

During the next 11 years, there would be 26 babies saved from abortion during 40 Days for Life efforts in Colorado Springs, and over 16,000 babies saved across the country and world. We know of one abortion worker who quit in Colorado Springs and over 191 around the world. 104 abortion centers have closed around the world. There have been at least 1,000 participants here in Colorado Springs and over a million across the world, all standing up for life. We hope and pray for the day when abortion is not only illegal but unthinkable.

One of the miracles of 40 Days for Life is how God works on our own hearts as we go to Him in prayer on the sidewalk. I know of people who were away from the church and were brought back after praying on the sidewalk. I know of a post-abortive man who received healing at the sidewalk. God works through us to save babies, help abortion workers quit, and help women and men find post-abortion healing, but he also works in us as well, to bring us closer to Himself and to heal our past pain.

Planned Parenthood is an evil place. Abortion clinics are satan's throne on earth where the bloody sacrifice of innocent babies happens every day. In stark contrast to this is the love and care shown by people who participate in 40 Days for Life, the Sidewalk Advocates, those who work and volunteer at the Pregnancy Centers, and all who reach out to help women who are in need. 40 Days for Life is one of God's solutions to this holocaust of abortion.

I truly see heaven touching earth in the hundreds of kind and peaceful people who have prayed at the sidewalk over the years near Planned Parenthood and all those across the world who give of themselves in the effort to end abortion and help women and men find healing from past abortions.

Reflection

Are you or someone you know pregnant and in need of help?
There are free pregnancy help centers available!

In Colorado Springs, contact:
***The Pregnancy Center**
Westside 719-623-2870 Eastside 719-591-2724

To find a pregnancy center in the U.S. or Canada, contact
***Care Net**
866-993-0794

Day 23

Spiritual Warfare at the Abortion Clinic

"Put on the whole armor of God, that you may be able to stand against the wiles of the devil. For we are not contending against flesh and blood, but against the principalities, against the powers, against the world rulers of this present darkness, against the spiritual hosts of wickedness in the heavenly places. Therefore take the whole armor of God, that you may be able to withstand in the evil day, and having done all, to stand. Stand therefore, having girded your loins with truth, and having put on the breastplate of righteousness, and having shod your feet with the equipment of the gospel of peace; above all taking the shield of faith, with which you can quench all the flaming darts of the evil one. And take the helmet of salvation, and the sword of the Spirit, which is the word of God."

Ephesians 6:11-17

I have experienced spiritual warfare at various times in my life, the most visual of these has been while praying in front of Planned Parenthood.

Praying at the sidewalk in front of an abortion clinic is not for the faint of heart. While most people drive by without a word, and some honk or shout words of encouragement, some people scream obscenities or give the sidewalk advocates and prayer warriors the finger. One time, a man was screaming and was so upset, he hit the median and flipped his car over, landing right in front of the people praying. He was OK, and (you will be amazed at the Divine Providence here) there was a doctor praying at the sidewalk when it happened. Of course, he went over to help the man and called 911.

There have been a few times praying at the sidewalk that I have been afraid but then chose to trust in God. One time a man came to the sidewalk when Fr. Bill was celebrating Mass. The man went behind us and was saying weird things. I think they must have been demonic. *"Well, if he kills us, we will be martyrs and go straight to heaven,"* I thought. (But I was still nervous.) At the sign of peace, we shook hands with him, and he left not long after that.

Love dispels evil.

"But pray unceasingly also for the rest of men for they offer ground for hoping that they may be converted and win their way to God. Give them an opportunity therefore, of becoming your disciples. Meet their angry outbursts with your own gentleness, their boastfulness with your humility, their revilings with your prayers,

their error with your constancy in the faith, their harshness with your meekness; and beware of trying to match their example."

St. Ignatius of Antioch—First Christian Martyr at the Coliseum

Another time, an angry man drove by and his attitude led us to believe he was very unstable. We prayed that God would protect us and he wouldn't pull out a gun or hurt anyone. God protected us from harm. We are peaceful when we go out to pray, and God keeps us safe.

"I am not afraid...I was born to do this." St. Joan of Arc

The persecution of Christians is increasing in our society. The respect for human life has diminished with the legalization of abortion and now the legalization of assisted suicide in some states. We must stay strong in Christ. We must put on the armor of God, as St. Paul tells us. We may not be called to the extreme of martyrdom in our time, but we may. We need not be afraid. God is with us.

"Do not be afraid. Do not be satisfied with mediocrity. Put out into the deep and let down your nets for a catch."

St. John Paul the Great

Reflection

How have you been persecuted in your own life for being Christian?

How did you handle it?

Take heart! Thank God for this, for Jesus said,

> *"Blessed are you when men revile you and persecute you and utter all kinds of evil against you falsely on my account. Rejoice and be glad, for your reward is great in heaven, for so men persecuted the prophets who were before you."* Matthew 5:11

Fasting is a necessary part of Christian life and a MUST for spiritual warfare. Fasting helps us to see what is important in life and what we don't really need. It strengthens us to do God's will. Fasting helps to get the focus off ourselves and helps us to remember to care for the poor and those in need.

- Faith step: Fast once or twice a week. You will see great blessings!

Day 24

The Mercy of God

"A voice was heard in Ramah,
wailing and loud lamentation,
Rachel weeping for her children.
She refused to be consoled,
Because they were no more."
Matthew 2:18

The dad played with his little son in the Planned Parenthood parking lot. He was throwing his little boy up in the air and catching him. They were having a fun time. Yet, the little boy's mom was inside the abortion clinic getting information about aborting this little boy's preborn brother or sister, depriving him of a lifelong companion and the love of a sibling.

Before they went into Planned Parenthood, they stopped their SUV and I gave them information about the free services at the Pregnancy Center. I said, *"Can I ask why you are going into Planned Parenthood?"* (That way I would know how to best address their needs.) The man emphatically said, ***"NO!"***

not just once, but two times! They continued on to the abortion clinic. Driving out of the abortion clinic, they stopped their car and spoke with Gen, another sidewalk advocate who was on the other side of the street. To Gen's surprise, they asked her if the Pregnancy Center did free abortions. She said, *"No."* They told her they were going to have an abortion. The father was struggling to support his family and couldn't see having another child.

Gen poured her heart out and begged them not to have this abortion. She brought to their attention the love they have for their son and how happy they seemed as a family. How could they abort their other child? Gen asked if they believed in God and asked if she could pray with them. They said yes. When the couple left, after praying with her, their minds had not been changed.

Gen knelt down in the grass and cried.

It happens a lot. We see a man and woman, a mother and daughter, or two friends, go into Planned Parenthood for an abortion. As sidewalk advocates, we try to stop them. We try to help them. We want to get them to the pregnancy center for real help, for compassionate care that is free. We know if they have an abortion, their souls will be crushed. Their lives will never be the same.

The pain of abortion is like no other. I remember years ago, a friend, Stephanie, shared with me that she had taken training to counsel women at the sidewalk. At the training, they had to listen to the cry of a mother who had aborted her child. The mother was going through post-abortion healing and part of the healing process was to cry out their pain and sorrow. Stephanie shared the recording of the cry of this woman with us so that we could understand the pain post-abortive moms go through when they realize what they have done. This cry was like nothing I had ever heard before. It was a cry from the very depths of this mom's soul. This was a pain and sorrow so deep; my heart just broke for her and all women who have been through this. I just cried. I still get tears in my eyes thinking about it.

There are so many post-abortive moms and dads in our world in need of healing. God in His great mercy is the only one who can restore these moms and dads and heal them from their pain. This is how heaven touches earth in post-abortive moms and dads. God can make them new. Our Heavenly Father will make them clean again and forgive all their sins. The mercy of Jesus will wash over them like a gentle warm rain and the Holy Spirit will come upon them so that they will be able to once again have a carefree spirit and feel unbridled joy like an innocent child.

> *"Purge me with hyssop, and I shall be clean; wash me, and I shall be whiter than snow. Fill me with joy and gladness..."*
>
> Psalm 51:7-8

Reflection

Are you post-abortive or do you know of someone who is post-abortive?
Jesus, in His great love for you and His great mercy, waits for you, His little lost sheep, to come home! Please, go to Him in confession. Get confidential help from a post-abortion ministry and be healed.

I am praying for you.

Local Help in Colorado Springs:
*Project Rachel—Catholic Charities
www.HopeAfterAbortion.com
Fr. Greg Bierbaum 720-348-9700
Rhonda Miller 719-649-6198

*Bridges of Hope—Life Network
www.boh@elifenetwork.com
719-355-1177

Caring Help Across the U.S.
*Project Rachel

www/HopeAfterAbortion.com/

***Sisters of Life**

www.sistersoflife.org/healing-after-abortion/

If you are an abortion worker, looking for help getting out of the abortion industry, contact: **www.abortion-worker.com/**

Abby Johnson was a former abortion worker who found the truth and now helps abortion workers quit and find new jobs.

Day 25

A Heavenly Intercessor, A Faithful Priest, and Many Good Friends

"More than that, we rejoice in our sufferings, knowing that suffering produces endurance, and endurance produces character, and character produces hope, and hope does not disappoint us, because God's love has been poured out into our hearts through the Holy Spirit who has been given to us." Romans 5:3-5

Heaven touches earth in ways we cannot even begin to understand. Sometimes what seems to be a terrible cross turns out to be a blessing in disguise. I know, because I've lived it a few times.

On March 27, 2009, I was in the hospital only a few minutes away from giving birth. A priest (Fr. Dan) came into the room and asked if Mike and I would like a blessing. (Yes, I had an epidural. Otherwise, a few minutes to birth, my screaming would have chased him away and I wouldn't be telling this story.) We said, *"Yes,"* and he blessed us. We talked, and he found out we were Catholic. He said I wasn't on his list of people to visit and that he usually didn't go up to labor and delivery. He told us that he found out about us from a man in the elevator. The man in the elevator said that a woman needed him in labor and delivery. I thought at the time, *"How can that be? The only people who know I am in the hospital are my parents, and two friends, Nicole and Ann."* Also, I don't know anyone who works at the hospital. (My friend Ann later told me that her mother, who used to be a labor and delivery nurse, said that priests never went to labor and delivery when a woman was in labor, so Fr. Dan visiting me was very unusual.)

Fr. Dan gave us Jesus in the Blessed Sacrament and asked if I wanted to receive Anointing of the Sick. This scared me a little, thinking that maybe God was preparing me for something difficult (little did I know, He was). Fr. Dan gave me Anointing of the Sick. We thanked Fr. Dan and he left. A few minutes later, I gave birth to a beautiful little girl, Eva Rose. After Eva was born, I thought about all that had happened and wondered if perhaps the person in the elevator was someone from heaven.

Two days later, I had a horrible headache that wouldn't go away. Four days after that, I had what we thought was a stroke. My right side went numb and I couldn't speak, although I was still aware of everything and knew in my mind what I wanted to say. Mike took me to the emergency room and they airlifted me to St. Anthony's Hospital in Denver.

**On a humorous side note, when they put me into the helicopter, I was strapped in a stretcher. The pilot was in the helicopter and had it running and the two paramedics were strapped into their seat belts. But, um...the big door next to me was wide open. Well, I didn't want to be rude. I mean, I'm sure they knew what they were doing, but...THE DOOR WAS WIDE OPEN!! I thought in my mind, *"Um...the door...it's kind of open...I'm gonna fall out...and DIE!"* I had this very graphic picture of the helicopter taking off and me plopping right out the door—SPLAT! Well, it turns out they did know what they were doing after all. The people who were outside closed the door and all was good in the world.

The flight was both scary and totally AWESOME at the same time. When we arrived and landed on the roof at St. Anthony's, all these young, happy medics greeted us. It seemed like one of those doctor shows on T.V.

OK, back to the story...I was at St. Anthony's for six days and had more of the same kind of "strokes" when I was there. They found two blood clots in my brain and put me on a blood thinner. They did numerous MRI's and couldn't figure out what was wrong. I kept having the episodes, but they could not find brain damage.

There were many downtimes at the hospital. I really got tired of watching episode after episode of "The Greatest Catch," but it was so strangely addicting. I missed my children dearly and my little newborn, Eva. It was scary since I didn't know from one minute to the next whether I would live or die. I didn't know what would happen with the blood clots. I did learn to put my total trust in God and eventually was at peace with dying.

On the vigil of Palm Sunday, I hadn't had any "strokes" all day, so we decided to go to Mass in the hospital chapel. So…here is the thing about a hospital chapel… I, in my naivety, thought the hospital chapel was for the people in the hospital. So, I went to Mass in the St. Anthony's chapel in my hospital gown. (Don't worry, my backside was covered. I did know to do that.) Needless to say, it was a tiny bit embarrassing to discover no one else there in their hospital gown. A light bulb went off…oh…it is mostly the FAMILIES of the people in the hospital who go to Mass, because the people in the hospital are, well, they are sick. Go figure! Oh well, I was glad I went, embarrassment and all.

At Mass, God spoke to me, and as the Passion was read at the gospel reading, I truly felt the Passion of Jesus like I had never felt it before or since. My husband wrote his experience of what happened:

"Saturday, we were very upbeat because Michele had not had an attack all day. We decided to go to Mass at the chapel in the hospital for Palm Sunday Mass since she was feeling better that Saturday evening. It was a difficult walk for her, but we got to the packed chapel, and a kind couple offered up their seats for us. They gave us their palm branches (as the palms were all gone) and we carefully sat to listen to the word of God.

"As the reading of the Passion began, I noticed that Michele started to cry. I asked her if everything was OK and then saw that

she could not answer me (even though she was trying). She was having an attack. I quietly asked her if she wanted to go back to her room. She shook her head NO and closed her eyes to listen to the Word of God. As I listened to the Passion of our Lord I watched Michele focus intently on the words, and I was overcome with sorrow. I began to cry and knew that God was speaking to us through the word.

"Shortly after the Passion was read, Michele was able to speak again and her attack was over. Before I stood to take Communion, I asked Michele if she was able to walk up to receive Communion. She was weak from the attack and slowly shook her head no. I quietly told her I would ask the priest to walk back and give her Communion. As I walked up the aisle, I was trying to think of the words to say to the priest, asking him to give Michele the precious gift of bread. Just as I bowed before the host, the priest knowingly asked me if he could take Communion to my wife. I nodded yes and he followed me back to give Michele what she so greatly desired.

"After Mass, we sat in our room, trying to make sense of what had happened. We know that God gives everyone their own crosses to bear and that ours is a little heavier today."

I got to go home the Wednesday before Easter. On Holy Thursday, right before Mass, I had another attack and went to the emergency room. I spent three days at St. Francis Hospital while they tried to get my medicine regulated. A neurologist discovered that the blood clots were causing seizures, not strokes as they had originally thought.

While at St. Francis Hospital, I saw Fr. Dan again and

asked him about the man in the elevator. He told me that the man was tall, had a large build, and red hair. (I know no one who fits that description.) I decided to just forget about the incident, wondering who it could have been.

I was dismissed from the hospital on Holy Saturday and got to go to Mass on Easter Sunday. I continued to have occasional attacks until my medicine was finally regulated to the point that I didn't have any more attacks (Thursday of Easter week).

On Saturday, May 2, I went to the Respect Life Meeting. After the meeting, a friend, Nicole, said that she wished I would have shared my story. There were a few of us still there and Mary asked about my story. As I told the story to the few people who were left, Mary said, "St. Raphael," and told me that he is the Patron Saint of Healing.

Perhaps God was telling me that the man in the elevator was St. Raphael. The name Raphael means "God heals."

"And Raphael was sent to heal the two of them." Tobit 3:17

I prayed off and on for years, asking for God to let me know for sure if the person in the elevator was St. Raphael, my guardian angel, or perhaps just some random person who was inspired to tell Fr. Dan someone needed help in labor and delivery. God let me know that it wasn't important for me to know who it was or how Fr. Dan knew to bring me the Sacraments. What WAS important was that my Heavenly Father came to my rescue. My Daddy in heaven was looking out for me. I don't know what would have happened if I had not received the Sacrament of the Sick. Perhaps I would have died in childbirth from the blood clots or would have had a serious stroke if God hadn't sent Fr. Dan to help. Perhaps I wouldn't have died and received the Sacraments was to strengthen me for the trial ahead. I am not sure, but thank you, Lord!

I do know that while this was a horrible cross to carry, it was also a blessing at the same time. If I had it to do all over, I would go through all of it again. Why? I received so many blessings and learned so much about God and about myself during this time. I was weak, helpless to what was happening, and yet God helped me to depend on Him. I learned what it was to totally trust in God. Whether He gave me more years to live or took my life then, I trusted that He knew what was best.

The amazing people who prayed for me and my family and helped us out really touched my heart during this time also. My older children and mother were just wonderful, caring for the other kids and the baby, and my loving, courageous husband helped me out immensely as he stood by my side, even staying overnight with me in Denver, sleeping only on a chair for many days.

"So we do not lose heart. Though our outer nature is wasting away, our inner nature is being renewed every day. For this slight momentary affliction is preparing us for an eternal weight of glory beyond all comparison." 2 Corinthians 4:16-17

Reflection

When have you totally trusted in God? Was it in a time of sickness? Poverty? Was it during persecution from a friend or family member? Was it in standing up for something you believe in? How did you feel? The words of St. Paul can bring great comfort in these difficult times.

"For the sake of Christ, then, I am content with weaknesses, insults, hardships, persecutions, and calamities; for when I am weak, then I am strong." 2 Corinthians 12:10

Day 25, Part II

Stations of the Cross - After My Sickness

1. **Jesus is condemned to die.**

   Jesus, I felt condemned to die in the hospital having strokes/seizures. I didn't know from one minute to the next if I would live or die.

2. **Jesus takes up His cross.**

   I took up my cross when I had to go to Denver and be away from my children, Jesus. I missed them so much.

3. **Jesus falls the first time.**

   I fell when I cried when they told me I had to go to Denver. Mother Mary, you know how hard it was when I had to leave my newborn baby and children behind.

4. **Jesus meets His mother.**

When my mother came to the hospital, I knew she was going through as much anguish as I was.

5. **Simon of Cyrene helps Jesus carry the cross.**

   Mike helped me carry my cross by encouraging me and staying with me in the hospital. I know he suffered much too. Thank you, Jesus, for such a great husband.

6. **Veronica wipes the face of Jesus.**

   A wonderful nurse, Nicole, was so kind to me when I was scared. She gave me comfort and stayed with me as long as I needed her.

7. **Jesus falls a second time.**

   I fell again when they told me I couldn't nurse Eva because of the medication I was taking. Jesus, You know, this is when everything hit me at once. It was so heartbreaking, I cried.

8. **Jesus speaks to the women of Jerusalem.**

   I found out Stephanie, my goddaughter, had died at 28 years old when I was in the hospital. We were heartbroken. She was a light. *"Do not weep for me..."*

9. **Jesus falls a third time.**

   I fell again when I got home from the hospital only to have to go back again.

10. **Jesus is stripped of His garments.**

    I was stripped of dignity a bit as on my second trip to the hospital they didn't seem to care as much.

11. **Jesus is nailed to the cross.**

    Knowing that I may have to go through this forever

and being depressed from the medicine was like being nailed to the cross. I lost hope.

12. **Jesus dies on the cross.**

    I felt like dying when I went through depression. Being on a certain medication, I even had suicidal thoughts, which is unlike me. We switched medicine, and it was better.

13. **Jesus is taken down from the cross.**

    After the medications started working, I realized it wasn't so bad and realized that I could deal with it with Jesus' help.

14. **Jesus is laid in the tomb.**

    The issue of all this was laid to rest as I gave everything over to God.

15. **Jesus rises from the dead**

    I was eventually healed of the blood clots and seizures. Thank you, Jesus!

Reflection

Have you ever meditated on the Stations of the Cross, relating it to your own life?

- Faith step: Meditate on the Stations of the Cross in your own life, relating it to Jesus. Just think of a period in your life when you went through a difficult time. Meditate and place what happened in your own life into the Stations of the Cross. This is very powerful when you are going through difficulties. When we see the utter hardships Jesus went through, it comforts us when we go through our own.

Day 26

The Crown of Flowers

"...Be faithful unto death, and I will give you the crown of life."
Revelation 2:9

As I sat in prayer in the chapel, I was distraught, overwhelmed, and stressed. I felt as if nothing I did was right, that I was falling short of everything in life, as a mother, as a teacher to my kids, just at everything. I felt totally bogged down like I was carrying a huge weight on my shoulders.

After Mass, as I prayed, I felt someone place a crown of flowers on my head. I believe it was my guardian angel. These flowers weren't your ordinary flowers; they were an array of different kinds and colors. Some were even transparent and full of light.

My first reaction was that I didn't deserve a crown of anything, especially with me putting God in second place in my life, which I had done over the summer. I then understood that this crown was to remind me that amidst all the stress and turmoil of life, I was to remember to relax and have fun. I felt that I was to give my burdens to Jesus who would carry them for me. I did so and I cried and thanked God. Who was I to deserve such a gift? He is so good!

So now, when I feel the pressure of life, I remember the crown given to me from heaven. From this experience, I learned that we do have responsibilities and duties, but God doesn't want our time on earth to be a living hell. We are supposed to be living a little of heaven on earth here and now. There is suffering in our world, but God wants us to have joy. Being joyful through suffering is a gift from God.

"Come to me, all who labor and are heavy laden, and I will give you rest. Take my yoke upon you and learn from me; for I am gentle and lowly in heart and you will find rest for your souls. For my yoke is easy, and my burden is light." Matthew 11:28-30

Reflection

I grew up believing what many people had told me throughout my life, *"God will not give you more than you can handle."* I believe that is a falsehood. God **does** sometimes give us more than we can handle. Why? Because in those times, we turn to Him. We totally depend on Him. He takes away our burden and carries us through.

Does life seem overwhelming sometimes?

God doesn't want you to be overwhelmed. Depend totally on Him.

- Faith step: Spend some time in Adoration and feel His peace and joy and remember, these crowns of flowers are for you too!

Day 27

The 4 Crowns

When life was overwhelming,
and I was overstressed,
I felt helpless and discouraged,
and my soul could not find rest.
God sent an angel to me to place a crown upon my head;
This crown was made of flowers, and tears of joy I shed.
This crown was given to me, to lighten up my load;
I let go of my burdens and placed them on Him,
just as I was told.
Sometimes throughout my life,
God has given me a crown of thorns,
When Luke was young, when I was sick,
when others looked on me in scorn.
These times they were not easy, thankfully they did not
stay.
God lifted up these burdens and happily sent me on my way.
In these burdens, I have found, the flowers entwined
within,

The thorns and flowers, He gave to me,
and my love I gave to Him.
When I became older—and wiser—as they say,
God gave me a crown of silver, as my hair began to grey.
But *"NO,"* I told Him, *"NO!" "I don't want this silver crown."*
"I'm not that old," I told Him; *"This will really bring me down."*
"But dear child," He said with love,
"You are not old in my sight."
"Your crown still has the flowers of youth
and you now are clothed in white."
One day my Heavenly Father told me,
a crown of gold I'll receive,
More glorious than I can imagine,
if I love Him and believe.
"I do love and believe," I say, giving my heart to Him,
"and forever I want to be with You, when my light on earth goes dim."
Blessed Father, Son, and Spirit, one God and persons three,
I love and thank you so, so much for the crowns you gave to me.

It was my understanding that these crowns are given to everyone throughout their lives, most people are just not aware of them. I think I was given this gift/meditation to remind people that they are there.

The crown of flowers represents youth, joy, a carefree spirit, childlike trust in God, and purity.

The crown of thorns represents the trials in life, pain and suffering, loneliness, addictions, past hurts, and other trials.

The silver crown represents maturity, wisdom, grace, patience, endurance, and trust in God. These crowns can all be interwoven at times (flowers, thorns, silver).

And the crown of gold is what we receive in heaven. I can't tell you what that is like.

Reflection

Think of the crowns God gives us.
What crown(s) do you wear today?

Day 28

Helping Aunt Louise -- Intercessory Prayer

"...The prayer of a righteous man has great power in its effects." James 5:16

As we were praying for Aunt Louise one night, I asked the kids to picture themselves by her hospital bed as well as their angels. I did the same. There was a picture that came to mind. Aunt Louise was lying there, and I saw a person or creature cover her with some kind of plastic covering over her body. I thought it was an angel, but then an ugly spirit appeared. It was so ugly! I was scared at first, hoping that it wasn't the spirit of my aunt—she is such a kind, giving person—I couldn't imagine that. The face of the horrible, ugly spirit looked right at me and disappeared. Then I saw the plastic or covering being taken off of her—the opposite way that it was put on. It came off at her feet all the way to her head. I then saw a good spirit and it all got a little fuzzy. (I think my prayer was distracted by the kids at that point.) I understood that the demon was trying to take her soul. It was angry because I (and especially the kids) were praying. I saw her in a white robe. It changed to red and she received a crown of thorns. I took that to know she was in purgatory.

This was an amazing vision that God gave me. I realized how important it is to pray for those who are dying. This is the last moment that satan has to steal our souls and he does all he can to get the dying to despair or turn from God. Our prayers made a big difference!

"For I am sure that neither death, nor life, nor angels, nor principalities, nor things present, nor things to come, nor powers, nor height, nor depth, nor anything else in all creation, will be able to separate us from the love of God in Christ Jesus our Lord."

Romans 8:38-39

Reflection

Who do you know that has died?

Remember to pray for those who are dying and have died.

The church teaches us about the church triumphant (those already in heaven), the church militant (those of us still on earth), and the church suffering (the souls in purgatory). We are one in Christ, working together.

- Faith step: Find out more about the church teachings on these and other tenants of the faith. Some good Catholic sources to go through are Dynamic Catholic, EWTN, and Ascension Press.

Day 29

Trip of a Lifetime -- Pilgrims on a Journey

"But our commonwealth is in heaven, and from it we await a savior, the Lord Jesus Christ." Philippians 3:20

We are all on a pilgrimage, a journey, searching for God. God is calling us to Him, but He won't do all the work. We must search for Him. We must seek Him out.

"Ask, and it will be given you; seek, and you will find; knock, and it will be opened to you. For everyone who asks receives, and he who seeks finds, and to him who knocks it will be opened." Matthew 7:7-8

In 2014, I was absolutely blessed by God and my sister Kathy to be able to take a trip to Italy with her two daughters and my own daughter Emmalee on a pilgrimage with others. This pilgrimage was truly a gift from God. I felt the love of

God in many ways.

Here are some moments that made me cry or brought tears to my eyes:

*We went to Padua and I got to touch the tomb of St. Anthony. People had put prayers and thank you notes on his tomb. I read some of the notes; some were prayers for healing for little children, some were thank you's for prayers answered. God touched my heart so much for all these people, for the little children in need of healing, for the moms who had lost children, and for others who were pleading to St. Anthony to intercede for their loved ones. I started crying. Strangers were looking at me like I was weird, but it really touched me.

*In LaVerna, the place St. Francis received the stigmata, we walked through one door out to nature, and the absolute splendor and beauty of nature just took my breath away! I thanked God for the absolute beauty of His creation.

*We prayed the rosary at the Vatican, waiting for the pope. There was commotion and people talking all around, but while praying the rosary with a few people, my heart was filled with peace and joy.

*We celebrated Mass in St. Peter's Basilica. Wow. God is amazing! My heart will never be the same.

*As an art major in college, finally seeing the Pieta really touched me. Michelangelo's heart truly went into this.

*I absolutely loved this whole trip and being with Kathy, Emmalee, Kayla, and Megan. I love my family!

Other "Wow" moments...

*David!

*Seeing the Alps from the plane

*Riding in the Gondolas in Venice

*Touching the wall of the Coliseum was life-changing. I thanked the martyrs who gave their all.

*The basilicas and cathedrals were breathtaking! Some of these cathedrals took six centuries to build (The Duomo in Milan), six centuries! In our fast-paced, instant gratification society, we can't even comprehend this. When I touched the walls of St. Paul's I thanked the men who put such hard work into this and never got to see the finished basilica. They did it for the glory of God. That is love of God. That is love of your neighbor.

*Seeing the tomb of St. John Paul the Great

*Seeing the uncorrupt bodies of St. Clare and Pope St. John XXIII

*Going into the Pantheon, now St. Mary and the Martyrs Church

*The food, especially gelato, and fun times like running in the pouring rain were amazing. Who says you can't be child-like when you are older?

*Making new friends

"The world is a book and those who do not travel read only a page."

St. Augustine

Reflection

I have written here about physical travel, but we also can travel in the unseen world of the soul.

There is a special quiet place deep in our hearts where God calls us to, a place of peace, a place where we take refuge in times of turmoil, a place where we find the joy the world cannot give. In this place deep within our hearts, we rest in the Sacred Heart of Jesus, us in Him, He in us. When we find this place, no evil can overtake us, no darkness can overpower us, as long as we are one with Him.

What travel adventures has God blessed you with?

What journeys has He taken you on within your own heart?

Call on Him. Continually seek Him out.

Day 30

A Path to Holiness -- Daily Mass

"When He was at table with them, He took the bread and blessed and broke it, and gave it to them. And their eyes were opened and they recognized Him; and he vanished out of their sight." Luke 24:30-31

When I was in my late 20's, I felt a call to go to daily Mass, at least two extra times a week. As I attended Mass, my love for God grew. As the years passed, I came to realize from experience that if I only went on Sundays, I literally did not have the love I needed to give my family. It was so difficult taking care of two, and then three, four, five, six, seven, eight, and nine children and a husband. I didn't have enough love on my own to give them. I needed God to fill me with His love to have enough love to give to them.

At the age of 51, I felt God calling me to go to daily Mass. I didn't act on that feeling right away but waited awhile. After a couple of months, I couldn't put it off any longer. I felt a strong desire to do so, so I started going. I felt that God wanted to change my heart so I could be more like Him and bring more love to my family and others and help others more.

The first month or so I didn't notice any difference. I didn't feel any holier. (God must smile at my expectation of instant results.) I guess I thought I would turn into a saint overnight. In fact, quite the opposite seemed to happen. I was struggling with a new temptation. (You will hear about that later.) I kept going to Mass, knowing that receiving the Body and Blood of Christ would eventually change me.

Weeks went by, even months. This new temptation, why was it happening? The whole reason this new temptation began was because of someone I met at daily Mass. I kept having the feeling that I should stop going to daily Mass to avoid the new temptation; however, I knew it must be an attack of the devil.

After a year or so had passed, I noticed something. While I still struggled with that temptation and many of the same sins, I was trying harder to do better. I wanted to fill those sin-filled spaces in my heart with the love of God so that I didn't want to sin anymore. I basically wanted to push the sin out and fill the spaces with God's love. I also noticed that my journal writings were getting more in-depth and insightful. I wasn't just praying on the surface anymore; I was trying to get in deeper to know God better and know myself better so that I could be more like Him. I can truly say, while I haven't turned into a saint (ask my husband, he will tell you), my faith feels deeper than it ever has before.

I truly believe the quickest path to holiness is by receiving Jesus every day at daily Mass.

When hard-working King Louis the IX of France attended two or three Masses each day, his courtiers complained. His answer was this:

> *"If I spent much more time in following the pleasures of the chase, or in entertaining my friends at rich banquets, or in frequenting for several hours each day theaters and places of amusement, you would not complain that I was devoting too much time to pleasure. You forget, my good friends, that by hearing Mass I not only secure for myself innumerable blessings, but I confer the most important benefits on my kingdom, many more than I could possibly do in any other way."* King Louis IX of France

Reflection

Most of us don't have a dramatic St. Paul conversion moment in our lives, but our lives consist of many small conversions. God calls us nearer to Him bit by bit, day by day. If we allow our Lord to work in us, our hearts can be emptied of worldly things and are then drawn closer to Him.

- Faith step: Have you felt a call from God to go to Mass more often than once a week? If not daily Mass, maybe one or two extra days a week? God will bless you in profound ways!
- Faith step: Keep a Mass journal. Matthew Kelly from *Dynamic Catholic* suggests keeping a Mass journal. At each Mass, ask God to show you a way to become the best version of yourself. Then listen. Something will stand out at every Mass. It may be part of a Bible verse or psalm, a part of a song, something from the homily, or anything. Check out more here: www.dynamiccatholic.com/free-resources/the-mass-journal

Day 31

Climbing the Mountains

"...For truly, I say to you, if you have faith as a grain of mustard seed, you will say to this mountain, 'Move hence to yonder place,' and it will move; and nothing will be impossible to you."
Matthew 17:20

The day finally arrived! I was going to climb America's mountain, Pikes Peak! I didn't get much sleep the night before because I was nervous and excited. I got up at 3 a.m. and met Julie and Joe and we drove to the park where everyone who was participating in the Pikes Peak Challenge was meeting. We got our numbers and checked in. It was still dark outside.

We started up the trail with our headlamps on since it was still dark. It was so quiet and peaceful. It was really cool going up the trail and seeing little lights going up (everyone's headlamps). I felt like one of the seven dwarfs, *"Heigh-ho! Heigh-ho!*

It's off to work we go," I sang. The city lights were beautiful. The whole way up to Barr Camp was pretty easy. We were happy to have made it and we stopped to eat and take a bathroom break. We loaded up on gummy bears, which the event coordinators had, along with other healthier items. We continued on. As we got up about nine miles, I started feeling really sick to my stomach. I also felt so exhausted that I literally could have laid down on the ground and gone to sleep. I felt like throwing up, but I couldn't. I thought about going back down, but nine miles back down compared to four up, nope! Plus, I would have to say I didn't make it.

My mind got the best of me and I was looking for a way to give up, except I couldn't. I prayed. I texted Heather, an avid hiker friend, and told her what was happening. She gave me advice. I thought I would try eating something and Joe gave me one tiny pretzel, which I immediately threw up. Well, no more food! We got to the tree line and above it, there were just rocks and nothing else. It was like a desert. *"Well,"* I thought. *"That is appropriate because that's how I feel."* It didn't look very far to the top, but it was still four miles to go.

We arrived at a help point and I stopped to talk to the search and rescue guys. They checked me out and my oxygen was fine and so was everything else. They put me on oxygen and said it might help with my nausea. I rested and one young guy, Max, said he would go with me the rest of the way. He helped me so much. He was very encouraging and told me we could stop whenever I needed to. We got behind a group and it was easier just following them at their pace. They stopped and we continued on.

The weather was changing and getting colder. It started to snow little snow pellets. I tried to go faster. We got to the 13 Golden Steps (switchbacks) and I went faster. We were the second to the last group to be hiking up. (At least I wasn't last!) There was a thunderstorm coming in and it started lightning, super dangerous. Max said we could bunker down until the storm passed or just try to hurry fast since we only had ½ mile to go. We went really fast then!

As we got close to the top, I could smell the famous donuts. I was then hungry again and wanted to get one. There were a few people up there in the cold and snow cheering us on. We made it and a lady put a medal on me. Wow! What a feeling to know that I made it to the top of Pikes Peak! It was much harder than I thought it would be, but I made it! Julie and Joe were up there, and they greeted me. They had gone on ahead when they saw that Max went with me and made it up 15 minutes faster than we did. The whole climb, which I thought we could do in nine hours, took 11. (I never got that donut by the way.)

What did I learn from all this? Well, it reminded me of giving birth. I know, that's kind of a strange comparison, but when you are giving birth no one can do it for you, but people are there to support you. (It's like the support that Sam gives Frodo in *The Lord of the Rings.* One of my favorite parts of the movie is when Frodo was exhausted from the burden of the ring and the long journey and he just couldn't go on. Sam says, *"Come on, Mr. Frodo, I can't carry it for you...but I can carry you!"* We need the support of others to help us through.)

While I was climbing Pikes Peak, I really wanted to give up. I wanted to lie down on the ground and go to sleep. I prayed and prayed to God to help me when I felt so horrible. I didn't feel anything from Him. Did He desert me? No, God wouldn't desert me. I wanted to feel a bit of encouragement from Him though. Nothing. I kept asking myself how I was going to make it. Couldn't someone just come get me? Once again, no one could do it for me, but God did send people to help me. Joe and Julie helped me. Max helped me. Heather, who I texted, helped me, and all those who were praying for us helped me. Once I got past the mental block that I couldn't do it, I was fine. Yes, my stomach still hurt, and I still had two or three miles to go, but I could see the top of the mountain and I was going to make it. And I did!

It was surprising to me that tackling a mountain wasn't so much about conquering the mountain. It was about conquering my own mind and my own limitations. Of course, I did need to be in shape to do it, but 99% of this effort was in my head.

I know sometime in my life in the future when I go through tough things, I am going to look back at this and remember. Hopefully, I will look back at this time and other times when I have gone through very difficult things and have made it through, and it will help me to make it through once again, trusting in God, even when I don't feel His presence.

"The way Jesus shows you is not easy. Rather, it is like a path winding up a mountain. Do not lose heart! The steeper the road, the

faster it rises towards ever wider horizons." Saint Pope John Paul the Great

Reflection

I wonder, how much do we limit ourselves in life? How much is there that we have already decided that we can't do? We need to break through that mindset of limitations. God doesn't limit us, why should we?

What limitations have you put on yourself? How can you break through?

Go climb that mountain, whatever mountain it is in life!

"I can do all things in Him who strengthens me."

Philippians 4:13

Day 32

A Kiss from a TSA Agent

"Let brotherly love continue. Do not neglect to show hospitality to strangers, for thereby some have entertained angels unawares."
Hebrews 13:1-2

Stacie, Gen, and I were on our way home from Houston. We had just been to the 40 Days for Life Leader Symposium and our hearts were on fire with love from the Holy Spirit. The stories and witness of other pro-life leaders across the country filled us with hope and inspiration for the future. We were ready to do what God was calling us to do.

I got through security at the airport, but it was taking Stacie longer than Gen and me. I looked up and, oh dear, she had been stopped by a TSA agent. Something in her carry-on bag triggered an inspection. I waited a bit and then went over to see what was going on. Stacie, Gen, and the agent were having quite an animated conversation. It seemed that the TSA agent noticed the 40 Days for Life flyers Stacie had in her luggage. That wasn't what triggered the stop, but when he saw the flyers, a conversation progressed, about 40 Days for Life, the world around us, and so on. He told us he was Catholic and very faithful to the church. We really made a connection with this young man and talked with him for quite a while. This kind of surprised me because most TSA agents I had come across in the past seemed so stuffy and strict, just doing their jobs, and getting people through the line as quickly as possible. This young man was just filled with the love of Christ. (It goes to show how, no matter where a person works, or what their job in life is, they can bring the love of Christ to others.)

This TSA agent looked Hispanic but was probably from France or Canada with his French accent. As it was time to say goodbye, he gave each of us a big hug and kiss on the cheek. It was truly touching. Why? That innocent kiss said to me, *"I care." "We are family." "I am happy I met you."* I truly felt Jesus in this young man.

I pondered on this happening afterward. Why did this affect me so much? I came to this conclusion: In a world where we are so disconnected from strangers, in a world where we often don't show affection, in a world where we go through the lines of life in a hurry, ignoring the strangers who are standing in line with us, this young man stood out from the crowd. In that busy, crowded airport, with everyone rushing to where they were going, he cared enough to take time to talk with us. He cared enough to share his story and to learn more about us. Heaven touched earth in this man, this stranger, who showed the love and the joy of Jesus.

Reflection

We can all learn a lesson from this young man.

How can we slow down, notice the people around us, and show God's love to the strangers we run into?

Even a simple smile can transform someone's day from horrible to good.

"Every time you smile at someone, it is an action of love, a gift to that person, a beautiful thing." St. Mother Teresa

How can you touch a stranger's life today?

Day 33

The Word of God

"For the word of God is living and active, sharper than any two-edged sword, piercing to the division of soul and spirit, of joints and marrow, and discerning the thoughts and intentions of the heart." Hebrews 4:12

For some time, I had felt a nudging by God to be a lector at daily Mass. Thankfully, God is patient, because I kept saying, *"Maybe someday, but not yet."* Even though I had been leading 40 Days for Life for 10 years, I still didn't like being in front of people.

The way God works to touch our hearts is truly amazing. He doesn't ask us to do something without sending us an encouragement, either before or sometimes after we do as He wishes. What was my encouragement the first day I read? It was the feast day of St. Joan of Arc. You see, St. Joan of Arc is my Confirmation saint and is one of my favorite saints. I look up to her for courage when leading the 40 Days for Life efforts and in other areas of my life. On this day, the feast of St.

Joan of Arc, they were short helpers and didn't have a lector for daily Mass. I asked St. Joan to help me, as I was nervous, which of course, she did. (By the way, this particular Mass was also being offered for my mom and dad, another blessing from God!)

I had never understood why people would want to be lectors and get up in front of everyone and read, but now I do. Reading the Word of God was such a great honor and blessing to me. I can't even put how I felt into words. I felt a fire in me when I proclaimed the Word.

One day it dawned on me that when I get to proclaim, it is not just for the people in the chapel or church, but since all of heaven is present in every Mass, I get to proclaim the Word of God before God and all of the saints. Wow! Talk about feeling unworthy. What a blessing and honor it is to proclaim the Word of God!

Reflection

Did you know you can use the Word of God to replace any negative thoughts in your head?

Write down any negative thoughts you have. Then pray and ask God to show you Bible verses that will replace those negative thoughts. Each time those thoughts return to your head, recall the Bible verse.

For example, if you struggle with not feeling worthy, replace that thought with:

"Are not five sparrows sold for two pennies? And not one of them is forgotten before God. Why even the hairs of your head are all numbered. Fear not; you are of more value than many sparrows." Luke 12:6-7

If you struggle with not feeling beautiful, replace that thought with:

"You are fair, my love; there is no flaw in you." Song of Solomon 4:7

- Faith step: Read the Bible every day, even if it is only for five minutes. God speaks to us in His Word. Find a good Bible study if you wish. *The Great Ad-*

venture by Jeff Cavins from *Ascension Press* helped me develop a love and understanding of the Bible.

Day 34

Father, Deliver Me from My Sin

"Brothers and sisters, I know that good does not dwell in me, that is, in my flesh. The willing is ready at hand, but doing the good is not. For I do not do the good I want, but I do the evil I do not want is what I do...Who will deliver me from this mortal body? Thanks be to God through Jesus Christ Our Lord." Romans 7:18-19, 24

OK, I hate to admit it, but yes, there is this one person I sometimes get jealous of. She is one of the most amazing people you will ever meet. She lives a very holy life and is a good example to others. She is not showy in her holiness; she truly cares for others and wants to do God's will. She has a bunch of little kids, takes them to Mass some days during the week, looks perfect all the time, and seems to have it all together, you know? Who has it all together?

I never wished bad on this woman. She is sweet and lovely.

Her kids are awesome. I prayed for them. I tried to be thankful for her wonderful example, but yes, I was still jealous sometimes. When I had a bunch of little kids, much of the time I felt totally frazzled, and I looked, well, you know, like I had a bunch of little kids. My oldest daughter refers to those years as me being "zombie mom" which pretty much says it all.

One day, I went to daily Mass at the chapel and she came in with her little kids and sat in the front row. On top of that, another person shows up who is another temptation that I was struggling with (you'll hear about that later). I thought, *"Oh God, I am trying to be good going to daily Mass and you send the woman I am jealous of and the other person I struggle with."* I struggled at that Mass. I even wondered if I should receive Communion, I felt so unworthy with my feelings.

I went to Communion and God later let me know that I didn't do anything wrong. These were temptations. I didn't act in a bad way. I resisted the temptations. God also let me know that I should not compare myself to others.

I think that God sometimes places certain people in our lives to make us a little uncomfortable or to spark our conscience. There may be areas in our lives where we are falling short, areas where we can grow. (This is different from comparing ourselves to someone else, which we should not do.) In seeing the example of holy people, something in us is awakened. In those times, we need to go deeper into our hearts to see what God is trying to tell us, to find out what God is asking from us, or find out what He is trying to heal in us.

The amazing thing that God brought out of this was that it did make me reevaluate some things. I talked to this woman one day and she spoke of how she didn't want to go to purgatory. She didn't want to settle for anything less than going straight to heaven and taught her kids the same. I thought, *"Wow, that is the attitude to have!"* I will have that attitude as well.

I discovered through this that when I struggle with sin, I need to look inside myself and try to understand why I struggle with that particular sin. What is missing in my life that is drawing me to a certain sin? What is disordered in my mind or heart that needs to be healed and redeemed through Christ?

This sin I have struggled with (and others I won't mention) has made me aware that I need to ask God for His graces every day. I am just as capable as anyone else of falling into serious sin and turning to evil. I know I should never underestimate the power of satan and evil spirits. They are cunning and devious, and they know what my weaknesses are. I have found that monthly confession has been a great help in aligning myself with God and in trying to conquer those sins that sometimes take hold of me.

Reflection

Former President Teddy Roosevelt said, *"Comparison is the thief of joy."*

Do you compare yourself to anyone?

The only one we should compare ourselves to is our former self. The one we should strive to be like is Christ.

Thankfulness for God's gifts in your life is a great remedy for jealousy.

Remember to pray for God's graces every day.

Day 35

Beauty Through the Eyes of a Child

"Let not yours be the outward adorning with braiding of hair, decoration of gold, and wearing of robes, but let it be the hidden person of the heart with the imperishable jewel of a gentle and quiet spirit, which in God's sight is very precious." 1 Peter 3: 3-4

Like some women, I think especially teens and aging women, I struggle with the feeling if I don't live up to the worldly standards of beauty, I am not worthy. I know it is silly. I know it isn't true. I know it is illogical. I know the heart is more important than looks, but those feelings sometimes come to me. In a world where women are judged by how they look, it is easy to feel down when you are surrounded by gorgeous images of perfect women. When I think in this way, I realize how much I am still in the flesh and how I need to empty myself and open myself up to God's grace in this area of my life.

"For those who live according to the flesh set their minds on the things of the flesh, but those who live according to the Spirit set their minds on the things of the Spirit." Romans 8:5

One day, little 10-year-old Luke touched my heart so much. I had just put on my swimsuit, and of course, at age 51, I was very aware of my flabby arms and legs, my baby belly, my stretch marks, varicose veins, etc. Luke just came up to me and in the sweetest, most innocent way said, *"You look beautiful, Mom."* My heart just melted. Wow! My little 10-year-old boy was able to look past all the imperfections I see and see the beauty in me. It touched me so deeply.

Another time, my 21-year-old son, Erik, sent me a video for Mother's Day of a remake of the song *"Isn't She Lovely."* He isn't one to send stuff like this but sent it just when I needed it most. I cried.

I know I shouldn't base my self-esteem on my own insecurities. I know I should base my self-esteem on how God sees me, as His daughter, made perfectly in His image. That, my friends, is a gift from heaven and true beauty.

Growing Older

The laugh lines around my eyes and mouth are reminders of the joy my husband, children, family, and friends have brought me.

The stretch marks on my thighs and my "muffin top" are badges of honor for carrying 13 beautiful children in my womb.

(And perhaps the result of a few too many chocolates!)

My wrinkled hands remind me of the times I have served family, friends, and strangers.

Each grey hair on my head reminds me of the tough times I endured that made me stronger and formed me into who I am today.

The pain in my heart from others breaking it reminds me that I am alive, have loved, and have been loved.

I will love my face and body just the way they are. You may see imperfections. I see daily reminders of the gifts God has given to me.

Reflection

How do you view beauty, from God's point of view, or man's?

"You are all fair, my love; there is no flaw in you." Song 4:7

Day 36

Redemptive Suffering

"As the outcome of your faith you obtain the salvation of your souls." 1 Peter 1:9

When Mike got laid off in 2009, we went through a series of difficulties, one right after another, that in our lives was unprecedented. This lasted over seven years. While it hadn't all been doom and gloom, and we'd had some amazing times since then also, the number of difficulties had been staggering to me. It started when Mike got laid off. Then I went through three major medical problems in less than a year, one of them life-threatening and one of them leaving me dependent on medication for the rest of my life since a body part needed for survival was removed (thyroid). God was with us that whole time.

The first time Mike was laid off, it was for over a year, yet miraculously, we didn't lose our home despite missing mortgage payments for a year! We had to swallow our pride and accept government help to survive, which was humbling and extremely hard to do.

Mike started a new job over a year later and they let him go after a year. He began another new job and was laid off after six months, began another, and was laid off after five months. He also had two heart attacks, one major. According to the world, he should not be alive after having the heart attack called "The Widow Maker." Marriage difficulties in all this? Of course! How can people go through one hardship after another and not experience stress and emotional turmoil? But God gave us good times as well, and Mike is a truly amazing man. He suffered through this, keeping much of it to himself at times. My question to God was always, *"Why?" "Why do we keep going through this?" "Are we doing something wrong? Am I not trusting You enough and I need to learn trust? Why is this happening?"* Sometimes the only prayer I could pray during this time was, *"Jesus, I trust in You." "Jesus, I trust in You."*

After years of seemingly no answer to my question, it came to me. It wasn't that we were doing something wrong; we were doing something right! God showed me in a split second that we were doing something right. Our sufferings were not wasted. We were participating in what the church calls Redemptive Suffering.

"Most Christians are not asked to make the supreme sacrifice, but God chooses some to participate in the salvation of souls, not by giving up their lives but by enduring sufferings that are over and above what they need for themselves. All those whose suffering is redemptive can say with St. Paul, 'Never lose confidence because of the trials that I go through on your account; they are your glory.'"

Ephesians 3:13
Mother Angelica on Suffering and Burnout

That brought much relief to my spirit, knowing that our suffering wasn't in vain.

"If God sends you many sufferings, it is a sign that He has great plans for you and certainly wants to make you a saint."
St. Ignatius of Loyola

Reflection

"Every pain we endure with love, every cross borne with resignation, benefits every man, woman, and child in the Mystical Body of Christ." Mother Angelica

Every one of us will go through suffering in our lives. When we remember that our suffering can be redemptive to ourselves and others, it makes it bearable and even a great blessing. (How many of us as children remember our mothers or fathers telling us to *"Offer it up"* when we were suffering?) Don't let your pain be wasted when it can go for the good of others.

Are you suffering in some way? Remember to offer it up to God for the salvation of souls.

"We love only to the degree that we are willing to suffer." Fr. John Hardon, S.J.

Day 37

Saints Among Us

"I therefore, as prisoner for the Lord, beg you to lead a life worthy of the calling to which you have been called, with all lowliness and meekness, with patience, forbearing one another in love, eager to maintain the unity of the Spirit." Ephesians 4:1-3

As a little girl, I once encountered a room full of saints.

Don't get me wrong, I'm not talking about saints who are already in heaven, but the good and holy people who we meet from time to time in our daily lives. When I encountered that room full of saints, I was probably around 10 years old. I was at my big sister Lisa's school Christmas party. You see, my sister Lisa is retarded. Lisa went to a special school 40 minutes away from where we lived. The first time I encountered her classmates, I could tell they were different, but different in a good way. The school she went to was for mentally retarded and Down's Syndrome children. When I walked into the school that winter evening, I was greeted by the happiest, most joyful children that I had ever met in my life. I was in heaven. From the very moment I walked into the school, the joy these children had was contagious. The laughter in the school rang through the air like the sweet bells of angels.

If we look closely, we will find that there are saints among us.

She had been diagnosed with one of the most painful types of cancer, bone cancer, yet my aunt Barbara Lynn bore it all with joy and love for God. Barbara Lynn was always a saintly person. I remember even when I was a young child, always seeing Aunt Barbara Lynn with a smile on her face.

One day, when I was on the phone with my dad, he told me that Barbara Lynn was in the hospital. He said that while she was in the hospital, she spent her time going from room to room, visiting the other patients to cheer them up and bring them joy. In her pain and suffering, she thought of how she could help others.

If we look closely, we will find that there are saints among us.

If her 101-year-old body would cooperate with what her mind was capable of, there would be no stopping this little firecracker of a woman. In fact, even though Evelyn's 101-year-old body didn't want to cooperate with all she wanted to do, her mind was still almost 100%. She spent much time in prayer and I always saw in her the trust of a child.

Evelyn called me one day, many years ago, wanting to get

involved with 40 Days for Life. Even then, she was impressive in her 90's. She went out to the sidewalk to pray when someone could bring her. She wrote Letters to the Editor and articles for the local newspapers. She planted a garden every summer. She got together with her family quite often. She was known all over the city; it seemed all I had to do was mention Evelyn's name to someone I knew, and they knew who she was. There were many things I didn't know about Evelyn, but I did know every time I talked with her on the phone, I felt like I was talking with a living saint.

If we look closely, we will find that there are saints among us.

"Sing praises to the Lord, O you his saints, and give thanks to His holy name." Psalm 30:4

Reflection

The word saint means, *"A person of great holiness, virtue, or benevolence."* A saint is someone who is set apart for God.

Do you know any living saints? How have they brought you closer to God?

Day 38

Overcoming Temptation

"No temptation has overtaken you that is not common to man. God is faithful, and He will not let you be tempted beyond your strength, but with the temptation will also provide the way of escape, that you may be able to endure it." 1 Corinthians 10:13

Mike and I have been through a lot. Marriage is wonderful. Marriage is also very, very difficult. To keep your heart open to someone who has broken it, again and again, is hard. To let them in after they are the cause of many nights of crying in desperation is very hard. I realized I had done the same to him, and I was truly sorry, but that didn't make me hurt any less. I had forgiven him all his past wrongdoings as I knew he had forgiven mine, but the hurt and pain lingered on. The bad memories were still there.

We had been married for 29 years, but the last eight had been the toughest. From illnesses for both of us to unemployment for Mike over and over again, life had taken its toll on us. Mike was beaten down and I was tired of trying. How could I lift him up when he didn't believe in himself? He was often depressed and spent a lot of time on the computer to escape. I also think I distanced myself from him somewhat after his last heart attack—not on purpose, but I think it was a defense mechanism to protect myself from being too close in case he died. It was not the right thing to do, I know, but it was done unconsciously.

In the fall of 2016, I felt God calling me to go to Mass every day. Part of this was just looking at how the world was falling apart. In our world gone crazy, I knew that God was the ONLY answer, the only solution. I knew my time on earth would be best spent going to God in praise and prayer at Mass, asking Him to heal us, our families, and our country and world. Well, whenever you try to get closer to God, in whatever way, the devil is not far behind, ready to attack where you are weakest. Where was I weakest? My marriage.

One day after daily Mass, I was introduced to Jeff (not his real name). Jeff looked a little younger than me. I only had a conversation with Jeff one time in a span of three years, but in my troubled marriage and emotional state, it was easy to be drawn to him and his kind eyes. I noticed a lot about him. He was funny. He was kind. He was peaceful. He was handsome. He obviously loved God very much and Jesus in the Blessed Sacrament. When I saw him put his head into his hands after Communion one day, just like I do, I was hooked. I knew I'd better stay away from him, because this guy, I could easily fall for. So, I tried to stay on the opposite side of the chapel from him when I went to Mass to avoid being tempted. (I couldn't control where he sat, however, when he came in after me.) A priest warned me not to do anything to get closer to Jeff, but the devil is very sneaky and tries to tempt us toward sin in increments when he knows we won't fall into it all at once.

Many times, when I looked into Jeff's eyes at the sign of peace, I felt totally drawn to him, and I didn't look away right away. He didn't look away right away either. There was a definite attraction, at least on my part. Was it the same for him? There were a few times after Mass that I caught Jeff just looking at me. When he saw that I noticed him staring at me, he didn't look away. I felt a bond between us. Maybe we were going through similar experiences that connected us somehow, I don't know. His eyes were so kind; I felt drawn in.

"The face is the mirror of the mind and eyes without speaking confess the secrets of the heart." St. Jerome

This was the first time since I got married so many years ago that my heart was so drawn to someone else. It was tough since my own marriage seemed to be falling apart and I longed for someone to understand and appreciate me. I longed to give my heart to someone who wouldn't break it again and again.

I needed God's help in a big way to fight the temptation to get to know him better. I was also tempted to stop going to daily Mass to avoid running into him, but I knew that was from the devil. In the Bible, it is promised that God *"...will not let you be tempted beyond your strength."* I decided that nothing would keep me from receiving Jesus every day, even this temptation. God would be with me.

Sometimes I wouldn't see Jeff for a month or longer, but the attachment was still there; I still thought about him a lot. What was he like? What was his life like? Was he as kind as he seemed? I was tempted to go talk to him to get to know him better. *"Maybe if I get to know him better, I won't like him,"* I thought. A priest warned me against doing this.

During this time, while I never ever considered being unfaithful to Mike, one priest told me that thinking of Jeff in this way was a type of emotional cheating. I needed to get my act together. I started going to daily Mass at another church on the days I was able to do so to try to limit the temptation.

A good priest told me not to ask God to take this cross from me, that God has a reason for everything. So how did I see heaven touching earth in this? Why did God allow this? This was difficult. It hurt. Was the temptation from the devil? Was it allowed by God as a test of faithfulness? Whatever the case may be, I knew that graces were being given to me from heaven to help me respond to the temptation. While I couldn't control my feelings for this man, I could control my response to those feelings, and therein lies either the sin, or the virtue. I needed to be totally dependent on God since I was torn between the sin of the flesh, thinking of this kind man who didn't hurt me, or the spiritual choice of giving my whole heart to my husband, even though I knew I would be hurt since true relationships do hurt. I needed to be vulnerable in my relationship with my husband, even though I would be hurt again and again. God would be able to strengthen me in my weakness and heal our marriage.

"Temptation is then a necessary part of life with God, something potentially useful and helpful to us." Spiritual Warfare by Fr. Vivian Boland OP

I truly believe this was a cross that God allowed to open my eyes to show me that there was serious trouble in our marriage, and instead of brushing it aside as we had done for years, we needed to take charge and do something about it. Perhaps I was seeing in Jeff what I was lacking in my own marriage. I longed for the fairy tale perfect relationship. But the fairy tale relationship takes work. Love takes work. Love takes sacrifice. Marriage is self-donation.

"Temptation usually involves struggle and difficulty, perhaps even blood, sweat and tears, but through such suffering we grow." Spiritual Warfare by Fr. Vivian Boland OP

I wish I could say that this was a temptation that was conquered quickly, but it wasn't conquered quickly. The temptation did contain a lot of struggle, difficulty, and tears. Even with much prayer, frequent reception of the sacraments, and fasting, I struggled with this temptation for over three years. I was finally freed of this temptation once I got serious about working on my relationship with my husband.

Reflection

Temptations can be good as they bring certain weaknesses to light that we may have been oblivious to before. The temptations help us see the areas that we still need to work on. As we conquer any sins that the temptations may lead to, we open up the places in our hearts where God is not yet King.

Do you have a specific temptation you struggle with? God is always there to help especially in frequent visits to confession, frequent reception of the Eucharist, and fasting.

As promised, God will not let us be tempted beyond our strength. He provides an escape.

Finally, to be Christian, to follow Christ, we will have our hearts broken, even crushed, by others in our lives, especially those closest to us. Yet we mustn't harden our hearts. Christ didn't harden His heart to the pain. No, He opened His heart for all. That's where we are healed, in the Sacred Heart of Jesus.

Day 39

From a Turbulent Storm to Clear Waters

"And be kind to one another, tenderhearted, forgiving one another, as God in Christ forgave you." Ephesians 4:32

The sun was shining, the waves were gently rocking the ship, and the deep, blue ocean was vast and beautiful, extending out as far as the eye could see. Yet, inside my and Mike's hearts was the opposite of the peace and calm of the outside world. Our hearts were like turbulent waves in a never-ending storm of sadness, bitterness, and anger.

It should have been a fun trip. The cruise for the two of us and two of our children had been paid for by Mike's employer, so there were no money worries concerning the trip. It should have been fun and relaxing, but it wasn't. Amidst all the beauty surrounding me, my heart felt broken. I didn't want to be there. It seemed like all the couples and families aboard the ship were so happy and having so much fun, and yet there we were, both broken-hearted and alone.

When we got home from the trip, we talked and realized how desperately we needed help for our marriage. If we didn't get help soon, we would be doomed to live the rest of our lives discouraged, disconnected, and maybe even divorced.

I contacted Alexander House, having heard Greg and Julie's story years ago. I knew that God had saved them when they were on the brink of divorce. I knew God was the only one who could save our marriage.

When our discipleship began with Greg and Julie, we were met with immediate results. Mike and I opened our hearts to God, opened our marriage to God, and forgave each other of our past sins. We shared with each other what our individual needs were and discovered the ways in which God was calling us to meet each other's needs. (I didn't even know my own needs before we did this exercise. How could Mike meet my needs when I didn't even know what they were?) We learned so much in just a few weeks' time, and as we prayed together each day our hearts were changed in a profound way. Once we brought God into our marriage in a real way, everything changed.

This chapter is still being written. God is working on our hearts and marriage, as we are, every day. The resentment which we both held onto for years is totally gone through the grace of God. I trust that God will make our marriage into the marriage He wants it to be.

The storm is receding, and clear waters are ahead.

"Love is patient and kind; love is not jealous or boastful; it is not

arrogant or rude. Love does not insist on its own way; it is not irritable or resentful; it does not rejoice at wrong, but rejoices in the right. Love bears all things, believes all things, hopes all things, endures all things." 1 Corinthians 13:4-7

Reflection

Some say the final attack of the devil is the destruction of marriage and the family since the family is a reflection of the Holy Trinity. We see this destruction in a big way in today's culture. Let us trust in God and give our marriages to Him.

Does your marriage need renewal? Start by praying together every day, especially the rosary.

If you need more help, The Alexander House is one resource. https://www.thealexanderhouse.org/

Day 40

Death is Only the Beginning

"For God so loved the world that He gave His only Son, that whoever believes in Him should not perish, but have eternal life."
John 3:16

Being with my dad at his death was one of the most difficult moments of my life, and yet it was also one of the greatest blessings of my life at the same time. In the hours and minutes before Dad died, I was seeing, and yet not seeing, Dad between worlds, waiting for Mary and Jesus to come to get him, waiting to see his mom and dad and those he loved who died before him.

The day before he died, all his children and many of his grandchildren made it home to see him. (He had received the Sacraments in the hospital the day before they brought him home.) When they brought him home from the hospital in the ambulance, he had a greeting party of his large family which spanned from the outside of the house to the inside.

It was a welcome home! (I can't imagine the great welcome he received in heaven!!) The EMTs set up a hospital bed for Dad in the living room. He was surrounded by family all afternoon and was never left alone. He dozed in and out all day, speaking to us from time to time. He kept putting his legs over the edge of the bed, wanting to get up. Mom told him he had to stay in bed since he was so weak that he couldn't walk anymore. One time he woke up and thought he was in his bedroom and was surprised to see he was in the living room. His mind was still very much intact, although he did get confused at times.

When everyone went to bed, I stayed on the couch, as my sister Chrissy and I didn't think he should be alone. However, none of us thought he would die in the wee hours of the morning the next day. We thought he had more time with us, even though one of his lungs was already filled with blood, the other one was filling up with blood, and his breathing was labored. One time during the night, he kind of woke out of his dream state and saw me helping him. He told me to go to sleep, to go to bed. (That is just like Dad. Here he was dying and was still looking out for me.)

My sister-in-law Laurie came out a little after midnight and said she felt like I shouldn't be alone. (I think she sensed that Dad would die—whether she was aware of it or not.) I am so thankful she came out. She did so many things that I wouldn't have even thought of doing, which I'm sure comforted Dad and helped his passing go easier. Laurie helped him by sharing stories and by massaging his feet. During the night, Laurie also promised Dad that she would tell everyone that he loved them.

Laurie called my brother Mike out of the bedroom and told us we should talk to Dad and tell him he could go. She thought he was hanging on and that he didn't feel like he could leave yet. I held one hand and Mike held the other and we told him it was OK, that he could go be with Jesus. I do feel like Dad may have been waiting for that since it seemed like afterward, the dying process happened more rapidly.

As the night progressed, we did notice a change that gave us the feeling that he wouldn't make it through the night. His lips were starting to turn gray. He wasn't moving as much, except occasional sudden bursts like muscle spasms.

During the final hours of his life, he would occasionally reach out, as if he were seeing someone there. He was kind of glassy-eyed part of the day, going in and out of perhaps past memories…perhaps seeing people from another world…I witnessed two times that he reached up with both arms, one of those times was when it was close to his death.

A few minutes before he died, his breathing changed. Sometimes he would stop breathing for it seemed like a long time and start again. I think he knew we were with him, but he was unresponsive to us at that point. His breathing was more labored. Laurie started sharing happy memories with him that she knew he would love, his gardening, his roses, the time she "trimmed" his lilac bushes, and other happy memories.

Right before he died, God gave us a great gift, not only for us, but for all who we would tell in the days, months, and years ahead. Dad started mumbling. We couldn't make out the words, but Laurie and I looked at each other in realization, *"He is praying!"* We then heard Dad say, *"Holy Mary, Mother of God, pray for us sinners, now and at the hour of our death. Amen."* Those were the last words Dad spoke.

God allowed us to hear Dad's last words as clear as could be. What a blessing for everyone. Up to the very end, Dad was praying his rosary. He was one with God, asking Mary to help him. We held his hands and prayed Hail Marys, five or 10 of them, I'm not sure how many. Then, it was like each breath was so difficult. I prayed one prayer over and over, *"For the sake of His sorrowful passion, have mercy on us and on the whole world."*

This was a very tough time for all of us. I pray that Dad was not fully aware and did not suffer. (Dad was a tough guy and never complained. I think he knew God was right there and was at peace with whatever death brought.) Laurie and I were both crying and with each breath, I just prayed for Jesus to take him. *"Jesus, I trust in You." "Jesus, I trust in You."* I prayed over and over. I couldn't understand why Jesus didn't take him. (Later, I thought that Mary may have prayed the same prayer to God as Jesus hung on the cross, suffering, for three hours. How difficult it must have been for her to see her son in such pain for so long.) It seemed like it lasted an eternity, but in reality, Laurie said it was probably only two to three minutes. I prayed and asked Mary to ask Jesus to take him and it was not long after that he took his last breath. Thank you, Mary! Thank you, Jesus! At the very end, his face relaxed. All was still, and we waited to make sure. We cried and cried.

We woke up Mom, Chrissy, and my brother Mike and we hugged and sobbed together. Ali and Heather got up and cried with us. Eva woke up and we covered Dad so she wouldn't be scared. It was heartbreaking to know he was gone. I felt sick to my stomach. We were all happy Dad was in a better place and no longer in pain, but the pain in my heart after his passing was so much greater than I had expected.

The hospice people came to check his vitals, and the funeral home people came to get Dad. That time was hard. I kept touching Dad's arm, knowing that the last big Daddy hug I got (since leaning over the bed hugs are kind of only half hugs) was a couple of weeks before when I said goodbye after visiting and went back to Colorado. He stood outside watching me go and I kind of got a strange feeling. Maybe he knew then that he wouldn't be around much longer. Maybe he thought it might be the last time he saw me on earth, I don't know. I just know it was a different feeling.

It was 2:29 a.m. when he died. We realized it was Good Friday. This was another gift from God. I think Dad would have felt so blessed to be able to die on Good Friday and share in the suffering of Jesus.

I miss my dad so, so much, but I don't miss seeing the pain and suffering he had to endure the last nine or 10 years, so I am at peace with his death, as I think all the family is at peace. He was a great man. He was a great father. He was an amazing example of how to live a life for God. In his working years, he was always kind to others and treated them fairly. When my grandparents died, I remember him only wanting one thing, the plaque on the wall with a prayer for the home. He said that as a kid, he would sometimes say that prayer when he passed it. What kid does that? Not most, I must say.

It is strange that this book that began with the death of

my grandma (Dad's mom) will end with the death of my dad. Is there a message in that? I'm not sure. It is something to ponder and meditate on when trying to find and understand God's messages and blessings in everyday life.

I can truly say, that after being with my dad at his death, something changed in me. I can't pinpoint what it was, perhaps a greater appreciation of life, perhaps a greater focus on what matters in life. Perhaps what changed was just the awareness that we are all going to pass through death and need to be prepared to meet God who may come at any moment of our lives. We all may not receive the grace of death as an older person who is ready to die, so we should always be spiritually ready to go to our true home.

As my dad now knows first-hand, death is only the beginning.

"He will wipe away every tear from their eyes, and death shall be no more, neither shall there be mourning nor crying nor pain anymore, for the former things have passed away."

Revelation 21:4

Reflection

How has a loved one's passing touched your life?

Are you ready to meet your Savior if He were to call you home today?

In memory of Clarence William Bieker who died on Good Friday, March 30th 2018

"I have fought the good fight to the end; I have run the race to the finish; I have kept the faith."
2 Timothy 4

All around me is joy,
The sun beaming brightly,
The birds singing their merry tunes,
New life being born.

Yet, in my heart is pain.
Loss.
Loneliness.
Death.

He is gone from earth,
My loving Daddy,

My hero.
My model of goodness.

No more warm Daddy hugs,
That make me feel protected,
Safe.
Wanted.
Loved.

No more fishing trips with Dad,
With peace.
Stillness.
And joy.

No more smiles from Dad,
Warm, gentle smiles,
Full of compassion and love.

All around me is joy,
And I will feel it again,
Maybe today.
Maybe tomorrow.

But today is Good Friday,
And I feel the pain of death,
And the weight of the cross,
Like never before.

We carry our crosses, as Jesus did, but we are a resurrection people because of Jesus. Easter joy is a reality for Dad and all of us who follow Christ.

See you in heaven, Dad!

Day 41 and Beyond

The Holy Sacrifice of the Mass -- Heaven on Earth

"And the angel said to me, "Write this; Blessed are those who are invited to the marriage supper of the Lamb." Revelation 19:9

My life changed the most dramatically when I was given the grace in my late 20's to recognize the reality that the Eucharist truly is the Body, Blood, Soul, and Divinity of Jesus Christ. It is my hope that countless hearts will be opened to believe in the True Presence of Jesus in the Eucharist.

To fully enter into the Sacrifice of the Mass, I sometimes picture in my mind the angels and saints surrounding us, joining us in worshipping God. A few times, I have felt the angels and saints present at Mass. I have felt my goddaughter, Stephanie (who died in her early 20's), at Mass. I have felt my dad. I know that the ultimate and most perfect time heaven touches earth is in the Holy Sacrifice of the Mass.

I sometimes ask myself, *"Why do people sometimes miss Mass to do more frivolous, less important things?"* My only conclusion is that they don't understand the importance of the Mass. The Mass is the ultimate time when heaven touches earth. During Mass, time stands still. We are in eternity. Past, present, and future become one. I stand in awe that I am there with all the angels and heavenly court to worship God. Time stands still as we offer the ultimate sacrifice of Jesus to the Father. Time stands still as we offer our small sacrifices to the Father. Time stands still as all of those who have died before us and gone to heaven are there with us worshipping. Time stands still at the consecration when our very God becomes our food for the journey. How can we even consider skipping Mass?

Yes, sometimes the Mass becomes a little monotonous. Yes, sometimes the priest is not very interesting, but if we remember why we are there, a new meaning takes place. We are not there to be entertained by a priest. We are not even there to get happy, feel-good feelings. We are there to offer to God the greatest sacrifice ever made, His Son's death on the cross. Along with this sacrifice, we offer our own little sacrifices we have made during the week: doing the drudgery of daily work, taking care of fighting, screaming children, or putting up with that person close to us who gets on our nerves. But we have so many blessings He has given us! How can we not want to go to thank God for all that He has done for us, for all the beauty He has given us, for His great love for us?

During the Mass, we get to hear the Word of God spoken to us. We learn the Old Testament and how the Israelites aren't so different from us, with their turning to other gods, being punished, and then turning back to God. We get to hear the life of Jesus and see by His example how very much He loves us and how we should be with our neighbors. We get to hear the letters from Paul, how he suffered and remained faithful to God through it all.

"If we really understood the Mass, we would die of joy." St. John Vianney

During the Mass, at the Liturgy of the Eucharist, the simple gifts of bread and wine are changed into the Body and Blood of Christ! This is where our faith is really challenged. Many people, even some Catholics, don't believe it since they don't see it with their eyes. But we can hear it with our ears! Do you want to know something interesting that I learned? In the gospel of John Chapter 6, verse 66 (Get it, 666, the mark of the devil?), the verse says: *"After this many of his disciples drew back and no longer went about with Him."* Why? Why did they leave Him? Earlier in the chapter, Jesus multiplied the loaves and fishes. The people wanted Him to give them bread that would last forever. He told them that He is the bread of Heaven. He said if one eats of the bread, he will live forever. The people asked how He could give them his flesh to eat and He later said: John 6:53 *"So Jesus said to them, "Truly, truly, I say to you, unless you eat the flesh of the Son of Man and drink His blood, you have no life in you..."*

The people did not understand and did not have faith in Him so many left. He asked His apostles. They stayed with Him. Of course, they didn't understand either, but they realized that He was God and we can't always understand the things of God, we just believe because God always keeps His promises. He told us He would be with us until the end of time and HE IS! He is hidden in the Eucharist.

"It would be easier for the world to survive without the sun than to do without Holy Mass." St. Padre Pio

Reflection

Do we fully appreciate the sacrifice of the Mass? It is good to meditate on this. Scott Hahn's book "The Lamb's Supper" really opened my eyes to what is going on at the Mass.

- Faith step: As mentioned in a previous chapter, besides going to Mass on Sundays, go to Mass during the week if you are able. If you can't go to daily Mass, try one or two extra days a week. It is only ½ hour long. You will find God changing your heart and life in wondrous ways!

How Can I Recognize When Heaven Touches Earth?

When I was first married, I often wondered what I could do to follow Christ and be a better person. I mistakenly felt I needed to DO something to be a good Christian and "earn" God's love; I just didn't know what. I discovered with God's grace, Mary, and the wonderful saints, especially St. Therese, that I just need to love. WE need to love. Everything else is born from that love for God first and then a love for others, the two Great Commandments.

Our Heavenly Father loves us more than we could ever comprehend. He loves us where we are, in all our weaknesses and failings. If we could feel His love, in all its intensity, we would die from happiness. Since God loves us so much, He doesn't want us to stay where we are. He calls us to grow closer to Him in our spiritual journey. It is a lifelong journey and, as a loving Father, He is very patient with us and lets us take baby steps. Often, we try to do better and fall into the same rut of forgetting about Him and His blessings. We are all sinners and can always do better. We mustn't fall into the trap of despair or giving up. God is pure love. God is mercy. God is patient with us. We are bound to fall, that's why we have the Sacrament of Reconciliation.

Throughout this book, I have made suggestions on how to grow closer to God. Do what you feel God calling you to do. From attending Mass more to weekly Adoration and quiet prayer times with God, reading the Bible, praying the rosary, and more, we can grow a bit closer to God every day. It is all about having a relationship with our Lord.

Remember, as you strive to grow closer to God, keep an eye out for new temptations. The devil will not be far behind in anything you do to try to get closer to God. Don't worry though, God will give you the grace to overcome any temptations.

In closing, let us not settle for purgatory, in the hopes of one day getting to heaven. God wants us to go straight to heaven! As Christians, we strive to be holy. We strive to become saints. We strive to change the world, one person at a time, starting with ourselves and our families. And when the day is done, and our lives are over, we want to go straight to heaven.

Let us live each day with our focus on Jesus and heaven.

God bless you! I am praying for you!

"Above all hold unfailing your love for one another, since love covers a multitude of sins." 1 Peter 4:8

"Let love be genuine; hate what is evil, hold fast to what is good; love one another with brotherly affection; outdo one another

in showing honor. Never flag in zeal, be aglow with the spirit, serve the Lord. Rejoice in your hope, be patient in tribulation, be constant in prayer. Contribute to the needs of the saints, practice hospitality. Bless those who persecute you; bless and do not curse them. Rejoice with those who rejoice, weep with those who weep. Live in harmony with one another; do not be haughty, but associate with the lowly; never be conceited." Romans 12: 9-16

Final Thoughts: Be Not Afraid!

Beloved, do not be surprised at the fiery ordeal which comes upon you to prove you, as though something strange were happening to you. But rejoice in so far as you share Christ's sufferings, that you may also rejoice and be glad when His glory is revealed."
1 Peter 4:12

As this book was going through the final stages to be published, all hell broke loose. It was as if demons were unleashed upon the world, filling the world with fear, confusion, division, and hate. By the time this book is published, it will probably have gotten worse. We wait and wonder what will happen next; we ask, *"What new tribulation is just around the corner?"* Only time will tell. Is the book of Revelation playing out right before our eyes?

It all began with the Covid-19 pandemic. In March of 2020, most states and many countries forced a stay-at-home order on their citizens. The citizens were only allowed to go out for groceries, medicines, and work **if** the work was deemed "essential." Essential businesses could stay open, but,

"Who determines what is essential?" we wondered. Churches were not considered essential and were closed, but abortion clinics remained open in most states. So, the worship of God, our Creator, was not essential, but killing babies was?

"Woe to those who call evil good and good evil." Isaiah 5:20

As countless people have turned away from God over the past several decades, God is allowing the evil choices that have been made to run their course. Do we really think 47 years of legalized abortion in America and the killing of over 62 million babies would not have consequences? The consequences are huge. Now, there is no respect for any life.

Killing and looting are now happening in the streets. Vandalism and the destruction of statues and memorials are taking place. As I was adding this last chapter to my book, they began destroying churches. How soon before Christians themselves are attacked?

During the Covid-19 pandemic lockdown and afterward, I continued to write in my Mass journal. I attended daily Mass online and then gratefully attended Mass in person when we were allowed to do so. When God inspired me to write something down, I did. Looking back on these journal entries, I was so blessed to see that God was speaking to me—speaking to all of us—in what we are going through right now. Each day or every few days seemed to be a direct reflection of what was happening on that day, something I needed to hear on that particular day.

Our Heavenly Father is telling us that He is there for us,

no matter what happens. We just need to have faith in Him. He is allowing these things to happen to bring His children back to Himself. Like a loving father must discipline his children when they do wrong, so must our Heavenly Father. It is painful, but it is a great grace to save souls.

Here are some of the Bible verses I received from the daily readings at Mass or Adoration that spoke to what we are going through:

"Do not, O Lord, withhold your compassion from me." Psalm 40:11

"Come, let us return to the Lord; for He has torn, that He may heal us; He has stricken, and He will bind us up." Hosea 6:1 (This was very comforting in the midst of the Covid scare—*"He may heal us."*)

"For behold, I create new heavens and a new earth." Isaiah 65:17

"Save yourselves from this crooked generation." Acts 2:40

"My sheep hear my voice, and I know them, and they follow Me." John 10:27

"Let not your hearts be troubled." John 14:1

"Abide in Me, and I in you. As the branch cannot bear fruit by itself, unless it abides in the vine, neither can you, unless you abide

in me." John 15:4

"The times of ignorance God overlooked, but now He commands all men everywhere to repent, because He has fixed a day on which He will judge the world..." Acts 17:30-31

"The hour is coming, indeed it has come, when you will be scattered, every man to his home, and will leave me alone..." John 16:32 (This reminded me of how many churches around the world were closed and we could not attend Mass in person.)

"I am going to Jerusalem, bound in the Spirit, not knowing what shall befall me there." Acts 20:22

"Preserve me, O God, for in You I take refuge." Psalm 16:1

"For God did not give us a spirit of timidity but a spirit of power and love and self-control." 2 Timothy 1:7

"Finally, brethren, rejoice. Mend your ways, heed my appeal, agree with one another, live peace, and the God of love and peace will be with you." 2 Corinthians 13:11

"Do you think that I have come to give peace on earth? No, I tell you, but rather division." Luke 12:51
(Sometimes, like with the two previous verses, Bible verses seem to contradict each other. They really do not. Here, I believe God's peace is with his followers and they are meant to

live in peace, but the division comes when people turn away from God.)

"And since they did not see fit to acknowledge God, God gave them up to a base mind and to improper conduct." Romans 1:28

"I will give you as a light to the nations, that my salvation may reach to the ends of the earth." Isaiah 49:6

It is efficacious to meditate on the Word of God here, or the Word received in prayer, to see what God is calling us all to do in these times and to receive the encouragement we all need.

The evil in the world today is so great, sometimes I think I am dreaming the whole thing. *"This can't be real,"* I tell myself. And yet it is real. The evil is so dark, so deep, so intense, but no matter how deep the darkness is, God's light overpowers the darkness. God's light shines brighter in darkness. It shines forth through us, through faithful Christians who are called to stand up for truth and the gospel and to call on the name of Jesus.

Christians are being purified right now. Do you feel it? During the lockdown, was your family open to God's grace? Did you grow closer and pray more? If not, there is still time. These are times of great mercy in which God is purifying us, purifying His church, and calling His lost sheep home. Will we listen? Will we allow Him to purify us? Do we see His love and mercy in all of this? His mercy is immense and immeasurable, but His time of justice will soon be here. God is purifying us to help us to endure what is to come so that we can remain faithful.

Remember, whatever befalls us, whatever evil comes our way, whatever trials we go through, Our Heavenly Father is in control. Be at peace; Our Lord Jesus has conquered the world. If we trust in God and follow Him, we will see great miracles, such as the world has never seen. Will we be called to be martyrs? Perhaps. Perhaps will not be called to be blood martyrs, but what the church calls "white martyrs," or those who give their lives for Christ and offer up their non-bloody sufferings.

One day as I attended Mass, there were two Bible verses that really stood out for me. It made me a bit nervous, but Our Lord says to have no fear.

"...do not be afraid of those who can kill the body but cannot kill the soul." Matthew 10:27

and:

"'Here I am." I said. "Send me.'" Isaiah 6:8

Do you see why I was a bit nervous?

We have nothing to fear if we are united with Christ. Will we suffer? Yes, to one extent or another. We must carry our crosses just as Christ carried His cross. But we do not even fear death! For we will rise as Christ rose. We can look at the example of our brothers and sisters, the saints and martyrs who have gone before us, to help us in this time. We can turn to Mother Mary for comfort and help.

Let us give our hearts totally to our Lord and trust in Him

about the future. *Lord, please give us Your peace, Your joy, Your love. Help us to do Your will in these times and help us to lead others to you. Jesus, I trust in You!*

"I have said this to you, that in Me you may have peace. In the world you have tribulation; but be of good cheer, I have overcome the world." John 16:33

CPSIA information can be obtained
at www.ICGtesting.com
Printed in the USA
LVHW020509150221
679326LV00003B/164

9 780578 849331